CANADIAN DISASTERS

43 TRUE STORIES

René Schmidt

Scholastic Canada Ltd.
Toronto New York London Auckland Sydney
Mexico City New Delhi Hong Kong Buenos Aires

Scholastic Canada Ltd.
604 King Street West, Toronto, Ontario M5V 1E1, Canada

Scholastic Inc.
557 Broadway, New York, NY 10012, USA

Scholastic Australia Pty Limited
PO Box 579, Gosford, NSW 2250, Australia

Scholastic New Zealand Limited
Private Bag 94407, Botany, Manukau 2163, New Zealand

Scholastic Children's Books
Euston House, 24 Eversholt Street, London NW1 1DB, UK

www.scholastic.ca

Library and Archives Canada Cataloguing in Publication
Schmidt,René
Canadian disasters / René Schmidt.
First published 1985 under title: Canadian disasters; rev.
eds. published 1999 & 2000 under title: Disaster!
ISBN 978-1-4431-2440-9
1. Disasters--Canada--History--Juvenile literature.
I. Schmidt, René. Disaster! II. Title.
FC176.S35 2013   j971   C2012-905508-5

6 5 4 3 2 1   Printed in Canada 121   13 14 15 16 17

MIX
Paper from
responsible sources
FSC® C004071

Every one of these sad stories of our history has people we will never know about, unwitnessed, who lost their lives in a futile effort to save others.

"…the greatest love is shown by those who lay down their lives for their friends." John 15:13

Table of Contents

Nature's Fury

Death on the Move

Medical Disasters

CANADA'S WORST DISASTER

THE HALIFAX EXPLOSION

The worst disaster in Canadian history occurred in 1917 in Halifax, Nova Scotia. It still remains one of the biggest accidental explosions in history — as big as that of a nuclear bomb. In a few terrible seconds, more than 1,600 people died and 6,000 more were wounded.

It was World War I. German submarines lurked underwater hoping to torpedo English and Canadian ships. Every major Canadian city was busy with the war effort, and Halifax was the country's largest navy harbour. Freight ships from all over the world came to Halifax to form convoys, groups of ships that crossed the ocean, guarded by navy ships.

On the morning of December 6, 1917, a French ship, the *Mont Blanc*, was entering the busy Halifax harbour. She was loaded with almost 3,000 tons of explosives — she was a floating bomb. A Norwegian freighter, the *Imo*, was leaving the harbour at the same time. The narrow approach limited the amount of space for ships to pass each other. For unknown reasons, the *Mont Blanc* and the *Imo* found themselves heading for a collision in the narrow channel. Sailors on nearby ships heard the exchange of furious horn signals between the two ships. Many stood out on ship decks to watch the excitement.

Big freighters are hard to steer and react slowly. Both ships tried to change course, but it was too late. The *Imo*'s bow rammed into the *Mont Blanc*, tearing it open like a pop can. It cut a three-metre gash into it and became stuck. When the *Imo* reversed engines, sparks flew, igniting highly flammable benzene that was leaking from crushed barrels aboard the *Mont Blanc*. The fire quickly burned out of control and the captain and crew of the *Mont Blanc* abandoned ship, knowing that the ship was going to blow. They tried to shout warnings of the danger but couldn't be heard above the fire.

For about twenty minutes the *Mont Blanc* burned fiercely as it drifted toward Pier 6. Curious onlookers from other ships and businesses in the harbour stood outside, watching it burn. Firemen arrived with hoses to prevent the ship from igniting the pier.

Few on shore knew that the *Mont Blanc* was an ammunition ship. But Vince Coleman knew. The railway employee also knew that a passenger train would be pulling into Halifax any minute. While his fellow workers ran for their lives, he returned to the telegraph and sent this message:

"Stop trains. Munitions ship on fire. Approaching Pier 6. Goodbye." Coleman's body was never found.

The *Mont Blanc* exploded with a shockwave that immediately flattened two million square metres of downtown Halifax. Metal, glass and wood fragments tore through the city like rifle shots. Many people were blinded, including children struck by broken glass from classroom windows. About 1,600 people were killed in the first seconds of the blast and 400 more would die soon after. At least 9,000 people were injured.

Most of the *Mont Blanc*'s steel hull disappeared, but large chunks of the ship flew great distances. Part of an anchor landed three kilometres inland and a door fell four kilometres away in another direction. A fireman was hurled a great

Halifax, after the explosion.

distance and landed unhurt but dazed, and naked except for his boots.

Witnesses kilometres away saw a mushroom cloud form over the city as smoke rose six kilometres into the air. The bottom of Halifax harbour was visible for a few moments as all the water was blasted out of it. Soon afterward, an enormous wave of water eighteen metres high surged back and did more damage, lifting several ships onto the shore, including the *Imo*.

The Halifax explosion was so powerful it shattered windows forty kilometres away, rattled walls and toppled bookshelves a further eighty kilometres away. It was even heard and felt in Prince Edward Island, over two hundred kilometres away. An American battle cruiser, USS *Tacoma*, eighty kilometres from the blast, was rocked so badly the captain was sure they'd been torpedoed.

Citizens of Halifax believed an enemy bomb was responsible and most people feared a second explosion.

Hours later, a terrible snowstorm covered the mutilated city with forty centimetres of snow, adding further to the misery and cold. But determined survivors started repairing the damage, restoring power and telegraph lines and tending to the wounded.

Naval ships sailed toward the column of smoke, and their doctors, nurses and sailors began helping with rescue efforts. By the next day, supplies of food, medicine, tents and coffins were being rushed to Halifax from other cities.

One of the first trains to arrive was from Boston, carrying not only much-needed supplies, but also doctors and nurses to relieve the overworked medical teams in Halifax. A year later, in gratitude, the people of Halifax sent a fifteen-metre-tall Christmas tree to Boston. That tradition continues today.

Haligonians rebuilt their city with pride, using the new science of urban planning to create a modern city from the ruins of Canada's worst disaster.

DISASTERS AT SEA

Canada has the longest coastline of any nation in the world. Hundreds of shipwrecks that have taken thousands of lives lie in the Atlantic, Pacific and Arctic oceans. Our inland waters, especially the Great Lakes, have so many ships lying on the bottom that hundreds remain unidentified. Each shipwreck tells a vivid story of loss and heartbreak, but no book could tell them all.

The following six stories are just a few of Canada's maritime disasters.

THE *TITANIC*

The story of the sinking of the *Titanic* has been told and retold, but it is a tragedy which still fascinates us.

The largest ocean liner in the world, the *Titanic* was specially built for luxury and safety. Its builders claimed she was "virtually unsinkable," but the mighty ship struck an iceberg and sank off the Grand Banks of Newfoundland on her very first voyage in 1912. Although the White Star Line lost its reputation as a luxury passenger line, her passengers, including many Canadians, lost much more. Over 1,500 people lost their lives.

The *Titanic*'s destination was New York, but one out of every seven passengers was Canadian or heading for Canada. Thirty-eight Canadians were among the first-class passengers paying a huge price to be aboard the maiden voyage of the most luxurious ship ever built. These included Charles Hays, president of the Grand Trunk Railroad, Harry Molson of the Molson brewing family, millionaire Major Arthur Peuchen of Toronto and the wealthy Fortune family of Winnipeg. Canadians also made up many of the second-class passengers. As well, there were also many Canadians and would-be immigrants to Canada in third class, sharing rooms in the clean but crowded accommodations of the lower decks.

Seven-year-old Eva Hart and her parents, Esther and Benjamin, were second-class passengers on their way to start a new life in Canada. Eva's father was going to open a drug store in Winnipeg. She recalled: "I was seven, I had never seen a ship before . . . it looked very big . . . everybody was very excited." Eva's mother had a premonition that the ship would sink. She refused to sleep at night. Eva's mother had heard people call the ship unsinkable. To her, calling a ship unsinkable was "flying in the face of God." Eva's father said that was ridiculous. "My father was so excited and my mother was so upset . . . The first time in my life I saw her crying . . . she was so desperately unhappy about the prospect of going, she had this premonition, a most unusual thing for her . . ."

For added safety, the *Titanic* had the most powerful radio-telegraph system available in 1912. But on the night of April 14, *Titanic's* telegraph operators were busy sending greetings from passengers and didn't pay much attention to the last of many iceberg warnings, telling of a field of icebergs directly ahead. Other ships stopped and waited to navigate through the icebergs in the morning light, but *Titanic* sailed on at full speed.

The *Titanic's* sixteen watertight compartments were yet another of its safety features. Each compartment could flood without water entering another part of the ship. Engineers calculated that even after a full speed ship-to-ship collision, the *Titanic* would float for one or two days. Nobody calculated what would happen if a long gash was cut below her waterline.

That night, the water was calm and the ship sailed under a curtain of brilliant stars. Lookout Frederick Fleet spotted an iceberg that they were quickly approaching. He hadn't seen the iceberg earlier because the binoculars were locked in a cupboard and nobody could find the key. Fleet rang the crow's nest signal bell three times and telephoned the bridge. "Iceberg, right ahead!" First Officer Murdoch ordered full starboard rudder, put the engines in full speed reverse and closed the watertight doors. It was too late. The *Titanic's* starboard (right) side ripped along the side of the iceberg.

Just after the collision, Murdoch gave the order to shut down the engines. By the time the ship drifted to a halt, the iceberg was out of sight. But it had done its damage: it had torn open the ship's hull below the waterline.

The collision was hardly noticed by most people on the ship. To some, it was a scrape or a nudge. Most slept through it. However, Esther Hart, who was wide awake, felt the bump. She woke her husband to investigate. When he returned to say that crew members were taking covers off the lifeboats, Esther knew her premonition was coming true. While Esther and Eva got into the lifeboat, Benjamin stayed on deck with the men, following the rule of "women and children first." The last time Eva saw her father, he was watching her lifeboat being lowered. "Be a good girl. Stay with mummy. Hold her hand," he said.

The RMS *Titanic* as she is tugged out of port.

Though the *Titanic* appeared unmarked, the lower decks began flooding, filling six of the watertight compartments. Ocean water was halfway up the mailroom floor when Captain Smith appeared to inspect the damage. With the captain was Thomas Andrews, designer of the ship for Harland and Wolff shipyard in Belfast, Ireland. Andrews was on the voyage to make sure everything worked to satisfaction. Busy at his desk until midnight, he hadn't even felt the collision. Now he was the first to comprehend the ship's fate. It was flooding in too many watertight compartments to stay afloat. He told Smith they had a few hours at most. They agreed to keep the fate of the *Titanic* quiet to avoid panic. Both knew that the twenty lifeboats the ship carried, although adequate for British naval law, could fit less than half of the passengers and crew aboard. They would need to call nearby ships by telegraph to come to their rescue.

Neshan Krekorian was a third-class passenger travelling to Brantford, Ontario. He felt the ship hit the iceberg and, minutes later, saw water flooding the lower decks. As soon as a gate was unlocked, Krekorian rushed up to the boat deck and watched the lifeboats being prepared. He saw women and children being loaded on, but was angry to see some lifeboats only partly full when they were lowered. Other men standing around, particularly those from the upper decks, believed their chances were good on this "unsinkable" ship. In the first-class men's smoking room, a group played cards, ignoring all that was happening around them. But Krekorian had seen how much of the ship was already flooded. When another boat was being lowered with room on board, he took a running leap and landed in it.

As the last lifeboats were being launched, water was already creeping over the forward upper decks. The ship's orchestra bravely continued to play tunes to help keep everyone calm, and in the telegraph room the two operators sent SOS calls. Emergency signal rockets were fired off, but the *Californian*, a ship floating just a few miles away, did not move from her position. As the water crept up, fights broke out. Some of the officers had to use pistols to threaten people. Eva Hart saw a boy being forced from where he was hiding in a lifeboat by an officer wielding a pistol. She saw the boy leave the lifeboat and then curl up on a pile of ropes, crying. She never saw him again.

Major Arthur Peuchen saw lifeboat Number 6 being launched with only one crewman aboard to man the oars. He told Second Officer Lightoller he was a yachtsman and able to handle a boat, and Lightoller allowed him to go on board to help with the oars. Major Peuchen was scorned as a coward in years to come, as were many other men who survived.

The "unsinkable" *Titanic* plunged to the bottom of the ocean in only two hours and forty minutes. In its final minutes, over 1,500 people remained onboard. Of these, hundreds had already drowned, including engine room workers, third-class passengers and kitchen staff trapped below decks. Those above decks, passengers and crew, climbed higher on the cold rear deck and watched the bow sink steadily below the water. Both Captain Smith and ship designer Thomas Andrews went down with the ship.

The odds of surviving favoured the healthy, the lucky, the strong and the young. The only chance for survival was to swim in the freezing water and find some floating debris to climb onto. At the end, there was a mighty shudder and a thunderous explosion as the submerged forward half of the ship broke off and sank. The rear section righted itself for a few minutes before it, too, filled with water. Then it slipped into the sea.

The lifeboats had rowed away to keep clear of the sinking ship and only a few returned to haul people from the water. Those in the lifeboats would never forget the sound of hundreds of frightened and freezing people rising in a continuous wail. Many shouted for help; some cried in despair; others called to family members, "I love you!" as they struggled in the cold water. Eva Hart remembered the silence after the pitiful cries for help had all died out, "as if all at once everybody had gone, drowned, finished, the whole world stood still."

The first ship to come to the rescue was the *Carpathian*, which had answered the telegraph and steamed through the night to reach *Titanic*. Her crew was astonished to find only bodies and floating debris and lifeboats scattered amongst a field of icebergs. The unsinkable ship had vanished. The *Carpathian* brought all the survivors to New York.

At first there was disbelief. Monday's *Toronto Daily Star* claimed "TITANIC STILL AFLOAT" and a later edition quoted White Star officials saying the Titanic was still safe. A Calgary newspaper said that the telegraph had prevented disaster; all passengers had been removed by vessels speeding to her aid. But by Tuesday the whole world knew the awful truth.

Two ships from Halifax were hired for the gruesome task of collecting the remains of the dead for burial. Hundreds of bodies, along with debris from the ship, floated in a wide area. About 190 bodies were recovered and brought back to Halifax. Other corpses that were badly damaged were buried at sea, tied up in weighted sacks and dropped overboard as a minister or priest read a funeral service. Special trains took relatives to Halifax for the sad duty of identifying loved ones. Many of the recovered bodies were buried in local cemeteries. The body of Charles Hays, president of the Grand Trunk Railroad, was transported across Canada in its own private railway car. People from across Canada mourned the dead.

Much information about the *Titanic*'s final hours could only be guessed at until Dr. Robert Ballard discovered the wreck in 1985. Since then, many deep-ocean visits have shed light on her end.

GREAT LAKES STORM OF 1913: CANADA'S FORGOTTEN DISASTER

The worst storm to hit Canada's Great Lakes took the lives of 244 sailors and destroyed nineteen large freight ships, twelve of which sank with all hands. Nineteen other ships were run aground. Nothing since has even come close to the Great Lakes Storm of 1913.

The *James C. Carruthers* was launched in the spring of 1913. She was Canada's newest and largest bulk ship, 170 metres long and able to carry as much freight as modern ships do today. Standing on end, she would have been as tall as a fifty-five–storey building.

As large and powerful as the *Carruthers* was, nobody dared called her unsinkable. Ever since the *Titanic* had sunk on her maiden voyage the year before, people were more respectful about the sea. And the Great Lakes could be just as dangerous as the world's oceans.

On the weekend of November 7, freezing rain and blizzard-like conditions were forecast for Ontario and Michigan. On the lakes, ship captains watched their barometers and studied the clouds. Most ships had no radios, but red signal flags were out in most harbours, warning of a severe storm.

Many of the large freighters set out, despite the warnings. To stay idle in port was to lose thousands of dollars a day. Besides, these huge ships had powerful engines and faced storms regularly. During severe weather, they would find shelter in a safe port or wait at anchor behind an island.

On the *Carruthers*, the captain was confident. His new ship was carrying a lightweight cargo of wheat that would keep her floating higher in a storm. The ship left the St. Clair River, heading north into Lake Huron. But two storms collided and formed what is now called a weather bomb. Two metres of snow fell and, on Lake Huron, the wind doubled in strength. Waves breaking over the ship's bow and foredeck froze solid, their heavy coats of ice leaving the freighters looking like bearded old men. The ships were already hard to manage in the driving wind, and now the additional weight of the ice made steering even more difficult.

The *Carruthers* before that fateful day.

After a brief calm on Saturday, the storm resumed and the winds became even stronger, crossing the entire lake. Ships tried to find shelter, but many were driven into shallow water. Some captains managed to turn the heavy ships into the wind to stay afloat. Other ships lacked the power to turn and began to run aground or capsize. One ship was tossed aground three hundred metres in from the shoreline. Waves came in groups of three or sometimes combined into monster waves ten to twenty metres high. The hurricane-force winds swept some sailors overboard, leaving them to drown in sight of their ship or a shoreline.

On Lake Huron, eight of the world's largest freight ships sank or broke up, drowning their entire crews. American Freighters *Isaac M. Scott* and *Charles S. Price* rolled over, the wreck of the *Price* floating upside down in the lake for days. American sister ships the *Argus* and *Hydrus*, carrying twenty-four men each, sank. The Canadian vessel *Regina* foundered, and the *Wexford*, a sturdy Scottish-built ship and survivor of many ocean storms, disappeared off Goderich. The *Wexford*'s horn was heard blowing a distress signal in the early hours of Monday morning, but nobody on shore could help. The *John A. McGean* took twenty-eight crew members to a watery grave. And Canada's newest ship, the *James C. Carruthers*, went to the bottom with twenty-two sailors, barely six months after her launch.

In Lake Superior, the *Leafield* and the *Henry B. Smith* sank with all hands, drowning forty-seven. In Lake Michigan, the *Plymouth* went down with eight men on board. And farther south on Lake Erie, the lightship *Buffalo* was destroyed, killing six people.

Most of the sailors' bodies were never found, and of the ships that sank, the wrecks of the *James Carruthers*, *Hydrus*, *Henry B. Smith*, *Leafield* and the *Plymouth* have never been found.

When the storm ended, almost 300 sailors had lost their lives.

There are still unsolved mysteries and heroic tales of this storm. Crew members from the *Charles S. Price* were found washed ashore wearing lifejackets from the *Wexford*. The body of a stewardess from the *Argus* was washed ashore wearing the engineer's greatcoat and the captain's lifejacket. What tales of courage and self-sacrifice are here? How many people were rescued once, perhaps twice, to drown anyway in the cold waters of the lake?

For weeks after the storm, families travelled to shoreline towns to try to find the bodies of loved ones. Only a few were found. A memorial gravestone in a Goderich graveyard stands above the spot where five unidentified seamen lie buried. The single word proudly and simply tells what these people were: SAILORS.

THE EMPRESS OF IRELAND: SUNK IN FOURTEEN MINUTES

Canada's worst single ship disaster is almost forgotten today, yet the facts about it are remarkable. The tragic sinking of the *Empress of Ireland* in May 1914 took the lives of 1,012 people. Though it happened almost 100 years ago, it is still one of the world's worst ship disasters.

The *Empress of Ireland* was a Canadian Pacific passenger liner built in 1906, one of the "Empress" class of passenger ships. After the *Titanic* sinking, there was an enormous public outcry about ships not carrying lifeboats for all passengers. The *Empress* had plenty of lifeboats. It also had watertight emergency doors that could close and stop a flood from spreading throughout the ship. In addition, the *Empress*'s crew was trained to deal with all sorts of emergencies.

The *Empress of Ireland* was steaming down the St. Lawrence toward the Atlantic Ocean with a full load of passengers. The *Storstad*, a Norwegian coal ship, was heading upstream toward the port of Quebec. Each ship could see the other approaching and steering to pass a good distance away. Meanwhile, a fog bank descended on the St. Lawrence River as both ships approached the town of Rimouski, Quebec. Although their testimony later denied any wrongdoing, either the captain of the *Empress* or the first mate of the *Storstad* made an incorrect turn while in the fog bank. There was no radar at that time so ships couldn't detect each other in bad weather. Suddenly, officers on the *Empress* saw the *Storstad* looming out of the fog toward them. The big ships couldn't avoid a collision, and the coal ship struck the passenger liner on the starboard side opposite the engine room. The *Storstad*'s bow ripped an enormous hole in the *Empress*, flooding the engine room. When the engine stopped, there was no power to close the watertight emergency doors. Water flooded the lower decks and trapped many of the sleeping passengers where they lay. Within minutes the *Empress* was lying on her side and sinking rapidly. Because of the tilt and the lack of electric power, only three of her lifeboats could be launched. The ship took on water more quickly than it should have because many passenger portholes had been left open for fresh air, despite rules against this.

The *Empress of Ireland*.

The *Storstad* was damaged but floating nearby and quickly launched its lifeboats, saving many who had jumped into the water. But only fourteen minutes after she had been struck, the *Empress of Ireland* sank in forty metres of water. Many of the passengers and crew who had been in the lower decks had no chance for survival. One hundred and seventy Salvation Army members who were on the ship gave their life-jackets to others who needed them. Only twenty-four of them survived.

The captain of the *Empress* was pulled from the water into a lifeboat and immediately began organizing the rescue of those still in the water. Despite the quick effort to save them, a number of passengers drowned or died of hypothermia.

One thousand and twelve people drowned in the St. Lawrence that night. Although 1,500 people died when the *Titanic* sank in 1912, the *Empress of Ireland* sinking took the lives of more passengers and remains one of the world's ten worst ship sinkings. Scuba divers have often visited the *Empress of Ireland* wreck, although the strong currents make it a dangerous dive. Unfortunately, many Canadians are unaware of this deadly Canadian shipwreck.

THE *EDMUND FITZGERALD*

When she was launched in 1958, the *Edmund Fitzgerald* was the largest ship on the Great Lakes, and the largest ship ever to sail on fresh water. "Big Fitz" could carry 23,000 metric tons of cargo and was as long as a seventy-two–storey skyscraper is tall. By November 1975, she had sailed almost two million kilometres on the Great Lakes.

On November 9, 1975, Captain Ernest McSorley knew that a major storm was being predicted for the Great Lakes region. On Lake Superior, only very large freighters like the *Edmund Fitzgerald* and the *Arthur Anderson* dared leave the port of Superior, Wisconsin, to go out in such bad weather. Both ships were headed toward the Sault Ste. Marie locks, and the two captains agreed to follow the Canadian coastline of Lake Superior in order to avoid the worst of the storm. Each ship had prepared for trouble. Officers sent crews to secure clamps on cargo hatches, and loose items on decks were removed or secured.

The wind increased to a steady fifty-two knots, gusting to seventy or eighty knots, tearing the tops of waves and sending the water from them howling onto shore, ships and men.

This was a large, rotating storm, the winds reaching near hurricane force. The waves they produced were not like the long ocean waves, which lift ships like bits of wood and drop them down again; these were shorter and steeper than ocean waves, capable of raising each end of a freighter and leaving the middle unsupported. The *Arthur Anderson*, as long as the *Edmund Fitzgerald* and a newer ship, emitted groans and shrieks as it was twisted by the wind and waves. The sounds made the captain nervous. The two ships pressed on in the unusually fierce storm. Gradually, the *Fitzgerald*, the faster of the two freighters, pulled ahead of the *Anderson*.

About 1 p.m. both ships passed through the eye of the storm and for two hours, things were calm. A warm sun and calm seas greeted them. Then the storm returned and the winds came from the other direction. From the bridge of the *Anderson*, Captain Cooper saw the *Fitzgerald* pass close to a dangerous shallow area called Six Fathom Shoal. Most sailors knew that the shoal was not marked properly on their maps. The dangerous area of unseen rocks was a mile further north than the charts indicated. Cooper told his mate not to go as close as the *Fitzgerald* had done.

A few minutes later, Captain McSorley of the *Fitzgerald* radioed the captain of the *Anderson* with troubling news: heavy waves had knocked away two vents and damaged a deck railing. The ship had a list (a lean to one side), and both ballast pumps were going full speed, meaning the *Fitzgerald* was taking on a good amount of water. A few minutes later McSorley radioed back he had lost his radar. Would the *Anderson* stay close to the *Fitzgerald* and use their radar to guide them across the lake? Cooper agreed, but he wondered if the *Edmund Fitzgerald* had hit bottom on Six Fathom Shoal and torn an opening in her hull. Cooper thought he heard fear in Captain McSorley's voice.

Waves coming in groups of twos and threes were hitting the ships. The first wave would push the ship down and the second would wash over its decks. Sailors were ordered off the open deck because of the danger of being washed overboard by a wave.

The waves were especially dangerous for the *Fitzgerald*. Its hull had been lengthened in recent years and sailors testified it acted unpredictably when under stress from waves. At 6:30 p.m., a deadly combination of two enormous waves put the *Arthur Anderson*'s main deck under four metres of water. Only the wheelhouse and rear cabins remained above water for a few terrifying seconds until the large ore carrier came back up, shaking off the water. Somewhere, a few miles away, the *Fitzgerald* took the same waves. Nobody knows how the ship reacted. How much water was in her holds? How bad was her list? The *Fitzgerald* was out of sight of the *Anderson*, though visible on radar.

On both ships, off-duty crews huddled in their quarters and talked away their fears. A young sailor had once asked the chief engineer of the *Fitzgerald*, George Holl, if lifeboats could be launched in heavy seas if a ship that size broke up. His reply was realistic: "As far as I'm concerned, I'd just crawl into my bunk and pull the blankets over my head."

At 7:10 p.m., the *Anderson*'s first mate radioed that a ship was passing to the west of the *Fitzgerald*. He asked how the *Fitzgerald* was making out.

"We are holding our own," said McSorley. Those were the last words to be heard from the *Edmund Fitzgerald*.

Experts would argue for years about what sank the *Edmund Fitzgerald*. She went down too suddenly to send a final distress call. On the *Anderson*, an officer was following the *Fitzgerald*'s progress in the radar. For a moment he looked away from the radar. When he looked again the *Fitzgerald* was gone.

What is known is that the *Edmund Fitzgerald* broke in half, spilling its cargo into the midnight-dark waters of Lake Superior. The crew of twenty-nine men never had a chance and was likely killed in seconds. Their bodies were trapped in the wreckage in 160 metres of cold water.

A few minutes later, the *Anderson* passed over the waters where minutes before *Fitzgerald* had last been, but there was no sign of her. Frantic searching and calling other ships on the phone revealed no large, red-painted bulk carrier. The Coast Guard vessel *Naugatuk* was too small to search the stormy waters off Whitefish Point. The Coast Guard captain asked Captain Cooper if he would go out again to look for survivors of the *Fitzgerald*. The law of the sea is that sailors will help each other. But a captain is also responsible for the safety of his ship and his crew. Would he risk it? The decision was difficult. Would his ship survive more of the storm?

Cooper agreed to go, as did another ore carrier, the *William Clay Ford*. Oceangoing ships tied up nearby refused to go.

A smashed-in *Fitzgerald* lifeboat was found 13 kilometres from the site of the sinking. A few lifejackets and other debris

The mighty *Edmund Fitzgerald.*

floated sadly on the lake. The next day another lifeboat was found, but no survivors. Not a single body was found.

In Detroit, Father Ingalls of the old Mariners' Church received a call from a friend. The lake freighter *Edmund Fitzgerald* had gone down in a storm. Father Ingalls went to his little church, long a prominent place of worship for sailors. In memory of a freighter's crew he had never met, Father Ingalls climbed the old bell tower and rang the steeple bell 29 times: once for each of the poor souls on the *Edmund Fitzgerald*.

RESCUE AND KINDNESS IN NEWFOUNDLAND

When the United States Navy destroyer USS *Truxtun* ran aground off Newfoundland in 1942, Lanier Phillips was thrown from his top bunk. In the dark, there was confusion as the ship suddenly heaved up and fell down again with a crash.

"Torpedo!" shouted a sailor.

"We ran into the *Pollux*!" claimed another. The sailors could only guess what happened as they raced for damage control stations. Those with more experience brought foul weather gear. Others showed up topside in lightweight clothing, a mistake they would later regret.

It was World War II. The *Truxtun* was in a convoy of

three ships battling a fierce winter storm off Newfoundland, heading for a navy base at Argentia. The two other ships, supply ship USS *Pollux* and destroyer USS *Wilkes*, were somewhere nearby. Visibility was barely 30 metres through the snow. To avoid detection by German U-boats, the ships kept radio silence and none of them showed lights, which increased the danger of colliding with each other. Only the lead ship, the *Wilkes*, had radar to detect the other ships and the shoreline, but early radar was so poor a cloud-bank could look like a shoreline. The other ships followed blindly. What none of the officers knew was that due to a navigation error, all three ships were way off course.

When the *Truxtun* ran aground, it had just received an emergency radio message from the *Wilkes*, warning it to change course. But the warning was too late. The *Truxtun* became stuck between two rocks in Chambers Cove. The ship began leaking oil and taking in water. Attempts to reverse away from the rocks broke both propellers off. The other two ships had run aground about ten kilometres away.

At daybreak, the officers of the *Truxtun* began organizing efforts to reach the rocky shore less than a hundred metres away. The wooden lifeboats were soon smashed to pieces by the heavy waves. Rubber life rafts were just able to reach the shore, but the men who dared go in them almost drowned in the oil-covered freezing water as they went. Lanier Phillips was getting cold standing around for hours and took a chance on getting to shore. "I thought I was cold until I hit the water . . . then I felt as if a knife had gone through my heart . . . The men on the raft pulled me onboard . . . we began to head for the beach . . . Finally we made it. I felt as if I had not slept for weeks, knowing that if I go to sleep I would never wake up again . . ."

Only twenty-four men made it across before the rubber rafts got stuck, trapping the 120 men who remained on the ship. The *Truxtun* was slowly tearing itself apart on the rocks. As the men on shore tried to find shelter, Seaman Ed Bergeron climbed the icy slope looking for a farm or a house, but found empty fields. He stumbled for kilometres through the mind-numbing cold until he finally came upon an iron mine near the town of St. Lawrence. The men in the mine house saw an exhausted, oil-soaked figure struggling toward them. "Can you help me?" mumbled Bergeron.

He described the wreck's location; the mine manager ordered the mine shut and sent the men with blankets and ropes to begin a rescue.

The sight of a destroyer jammed onto the rocks amazed the Newfoundlanders, but they set to work. Using ropes to descend the cliff, they found sailors freezing, soaked in oil and too weak to climb. Some of the men were already dead. Miners gave away their warm socks or coats and urged the sailors to keep moving. They built a fire and began to help them climb up the cliff. Others helped the remaining men get off the *Truxtun*.

A man spoke, in an accent unfamiliar to Lanier Phillips.

"Don't lie down or you will surely die," he said. Above the cliff, men with horses and carts transported the freezing men to the mine house. Women brought hot soup and warm clothing to revive the sailors, plus washtubs and soap to scrub the oil from them.

Phillips woke to find himself lying naked on a table in a warm room. A woman was cleaning away the oil coating his skin. She rubbed at his arm. "I can't get the oil off . . ."

Phillips groaned. "It's the colour of my skin. You can't get it off." He had never known kindness from white people and was sure that when they saw he was black, he would be mistreated.

"I want him at my house," she announced.

Phillips slept on her couch for two days and had to be spoon-fed. The woman dressed him in what little warm clothing her family had to spare.

Ten kilometres along the coast, the *Wilkes* had managed to free herself from the rocks and back away, but the *Pollux* was jammed onto a rocky ledge and was beginning to break up. Attempts to get ashore by lifeboat failed many times. Before long, the bow of the *Pollux* broke away and the metres-high waves threatened to wash the bedraggled men off the ship. Some desperate sailors tried to swim, but those who hadn't tied their lifejackets properly drowned. Others got dragged into an oily slick, choking and drowning. Of the one hundred or so men who attempted to swim to shore, eighty died.

After almost a day, the crew finally succeeded in getting a rope to shore and made a breeches buoy — a device like a zip-line — to get everyone off. This helped get them from the *Pollux* to shore, but now they were trapped on a narrow ledge below a cliff. The tide was rising and threatened to wash them off into the ocean.

Meanwhile, a sharp-eyed rescuer stood above the *Truxtun* wreck and spotted a second oil slick, not coming from the destroyer. He walked along the shoreline for hours until he discovered the *Pollux* and its trapped crew. Word went out of this second shipwreck and men from the village of Lawn got ropes to haul the trapped men up the cliff. They were joined by the tired miners who had spent the day rescuing *Truxtun* sailors. With bleeding hands and aching backs they ceaselessly hauled the men up the cliff. The sailors could only be taken one at a time. Some were barely alive. It took until early the next morning before the last living man was rescued.

Two hundred and three American sailors died in the tragedy, but 168 survived. Without help from the people of St. Lawrence and Lawn, most of these would also have died. Lanier Phillips never forgot the simple human kindness shown him by a white woman. It changed him from a bitter young man to someone with confidence. He began to stand up for the rights of African-Americans and in years to come, broke numerous colour barriers in the Navy and earned respect and high honours.

An inquiry recognized the selflessness and sacrifice of the Newfoundlanders who rescued the sailors and who gave so freely from the little they had. As a gift from the American people, a hospital was built in St. Lawrence, paid for by the American government.

COUGAR HELICOPTER CRASH

On March 12, 2009, Cougar Flight 91 was carrying workers from St. John's Airport over the Atlantic, 315 kilometres to the giant *Hibernia* drilling platform and the Sea Rose production vessel some kilometres further. The big Sikorsky S-92A helicopter had sixteen passengers and two pilots.

At 9:40 a.m., a mayday call was heard. Pilot Matthew Davis radioed that his instruments warned of "zero oil pressure" in the main engine gearbox, where engine power is transferred to the rotors. Zero oil pressure usually means the oil inside has leaked out and the gearbox could overheat and fail. If the gearbox fails, the helicopter cannot fly.

Remarkably, helicopters are able to glide to earth safely even without engine power. Pilots call this glide "autorotation." In autorotation, the pilot tilts the helicopter nose downward as the aircraft falls. The rotors spin freely as the air passes through them, like a maple key spins as it comes to Earth. Near the ground, the helicopter is "flared," with its nose raised upward while the rotor blades are angled to give maximum lift. In most cases the helicopter lands gently.

Davis knew he had to return to St. John's. He reversed his heading, reduced speed and descended to 240 metres above the ocean. He hoped they had enough time to return to the airport. Both pilots assumed that before the main gearbox overheated and failed, they would notice unusual smells, vibration or noises. But so far the gearbox and engine seemed to operate normally.

Still, the pilots prepared for the worst. Land was a long way off. Below them, the ocean was rough and stormy. Search and rescue craft were called to stand by. The passengers were told to put on survival suits and were reminded of safety procedures.

Without warning, the gears driving the tail rotor broke apart, causing the helicopter to veer to the right. Davis cut power and began the autorotation procedure. Unfortunately, the helicopter was too high and travelling too fast for a smooth autorotation descent. The main rotor turned too slowly for proper autorotation, and the big helicopter hit the ocean surface hard.

The collision caused serious damage to the helicopter and injured the passengers inside. The flotation tanks, which should have kept the craft afloat, were damaged and did not inflate. Very soon after hitting the water, the helicopter turned on its side and began to sink. It was still about fifty kilometres from the Newfoundland coast.

Robert Decker was the only survivor. Despite swallowing seawater, suffering the pain of a broken sternum and the sudden shock of the icy water, Decker managed to escape. "The helicopter was sinking quickly, port [left] side down. It was instantly filled with water . . . The next thing I did was reach for my seatbelt and I pulled myself out through the window. I didn't know how deep the helicopter was at that time. I didn't know what was happening. I had my hands above my head and I could look up and I could see it was getting brighter and brighter and I guess eventually my arms broke the surface."

Patrol aircraft soon spotted Decker, floating debris and another body. The helicopter was gone. Decker was rescued after eighty minutes in the water. His body temperature was dangerously low because his face and hands were exposed. He hadn't managed to put on the gloves and the hood of his survival suit and the suit had taken in some water. Just one other person, Allison Maher, had managed to escape the helicopter, but was lifeless when she was found. The bodies of the pilots and other passengers were recovered from the helicopter days later as it was raised from 178 metres of water.

Transportation Safety Board investigators found the helicopter gearbox oil had leaked out when metal studs on a cover broke. The helicopter flew for only twelve minutes after the gearbox ran dry. This surprised many people because helicopters operating over the ocean were thought to be able to fly for at least thirty minutes in such an emergency.

The investigators recommended important changes to helicopters and the way they are maintained. They also suggested helicopters never fly over seas too rough for their flotation devices and that survival suits be made safer.

The many benefits from the oil industry have made Newfoundland rich. But the human tragedies like this are too costly to be repeated.

FIRE!

Fires have taught us heartbreaking lessons over the years. The stories that follow tell of needless panic and death of children in a theatre fire; wildfires engulfing towns; fires in jet aircraft thousands of metres high; and fires so severe they permanently changed the look of several Canadian cities.

CANADA'S SADDEST FIRE

On a bright but cold Sunday on January 9, 1927, more than 800 children lined up at the Laurier Palace Theatre on St. Catherine Street in Montreal to see the afternoon movies. Although children under sixteen were supposed to bring an adult with them, many didn't and got in anyway. The entertainment was a newsreel, cartoons and two feature movies. For children in Montreal, it was a great way to spend an afternoon.

Admission was a quarter for seats in the main theatre, and fifteen cents for the balcony. Often too many of the cheaper balcony tickets were sold. Children who arrived late sat in the aisles.

That Sunday the movies were *Sparrows*, starring Canadian

actress Mary Pickford, and a comedy called *Get 'Em Young*. The children were enjoying the comedy when a boy in the balcony spotted a flame at his feet where a discarded cigarette had lit some paper.

"*Le feu! Le feu!*" he shouted. Flames began to rise from the wooden floor, and frightened children ran for the exits. Smoke began billowing along the ceiling, adding to the panic. Children on the balcony found that one of the two stairways was blocked. The doors at the bottom of the other stairway opened inward, making it difficult for children to exit. Near the door, just before exiting the theatre, a child tripped. Another fell on top, then another. Children rushing down the stairs pushed those ahead of them until, within a short time, the entire stairway was jammed with struggling bodies. The ones at the bottom were being crushed and could not breathe.

Fire Station 13 was just across the street, and firemen were on the scene within minutes. There was little they could do for the children already being crushed in the stairwell. Firefighters desperately chopped holes in the wall next to the crush of bodies, but in most cases it was too late. There were seventy-eight fatalities, but only two died from the fire. The rest were crushed or asphyxiated.

Adélard Boisseau, an off-duty police constable, was one of the first rescuers on the scene. Among the dead children he carried out of the theatre was his eldest daughter, who was supposed to be skating with friends. The bodies of his other two children were identified that night. The Quintal family also lost three children in the disaster. Alphéa Arpin, one of the firefighters, was sick with dread as he came to the theatre. He found his six-year-old son among the dead.

Twelve-year-old Roger Frappier could have been killed if it hadn't been for his quick thinking. Seeing his exit was blocked, he jumped from the balcony, breaking his leg but saving his life.

An enormous outpouring of grief followed the tragedy. Church leaders condemned Sunday movie watching. Strict laws were enacted regarding children under sixteen years old attending movies in Quebec. Building codes were also changed to make sure doors and stairways would not prevent quick exits from public buildings.

WILDFIRE! SLAVE LAKE 2011

Every year, wildfires threaten Canadian communities that lie close to our vast forests. Some of these forests are getting older and drier every year, making them more prone to wildfires. Pine bark beetle devastation also creates huge areas of dead and dry trees. In many provinces, forest protection workers regularly cut firebreaks through forests near towns. These wide paths are cut or carefully burned to create a gap so fires cannot leap from one tree to the next. Firebreaks are important in keeping fires from getting close to towns.

Slave Lake is a community of about 7,000 people on the shores of the Lesser Slave Lake in central Alberta. It is one of the larger towns north of Edmonton and is surrounded by dense northern forest. The residents mostly work in oil production and the wood products industry.

On May 15, 2011, several different forest fires were causing concern in central Alberta. One fire was about eight kilometres west of Slave Lake and another fifteen kilometres east of the town. Unusual winds gusting to one hundred kilometres an hour carried embers great distances, causing the eastern fire to leap over firebreaks and roads. Fire crews worked day and night to extinguish it, but could not. The local radio station gave residents hourly updates, and on the morning of May 17, they were advised to leave. As the fire came even closer, people were given no choice: they were ordered to evacuate. The highway out of town which had been closed because of smoke, was reopened until residents left. Only essential workers remained. Other nearby communities were ordered to evacuate, and almost 15,000 people left the area. It was the largest evacuation in the province's history.

Residents saw a completely red sky as they left the town. Fire crews were called in from across the province until there were 250 firefighters in Slave Lake. They made a brave attempt to battle the flames in town, but were forced back by extreme heat and falling embers.

The fire destroyed one-third of the town, burning four hundred and twenty eight houses, seven apartments and nineteen other buildings, including the town hall, the library, a mall, two churches and the radio station. Fifty-nine more houses in neighbouring communities were destroyed. Although nobody was killed in town in the fire or during the evacuation, helicopter pilot Jean-Luc Deba of Montreal was killed on May 20 while fighting the fire.

The remains of burnt out homes after the Slave Lake fire in 2011.

Relief agencies like the Canadian Red Cross were so overwhelmed with donations, they had to ask people to stop bringing goods to evacuation centres. A rental agency in Edmonton provided apartments for evacuees, rent-free for three months. All across Canada people sent cash and goods. Canadian authors donated their books to restock the Slave Lake library, and the government of

Alberta promised $50 million in aid money.

Investigations revealed that the fire was deliberately set, although nobody was charged in the crime. Insurance claims of $700 million have made this the second most expensive event in recent Canadian history, next to the ice storm of 1998. Besides the cost to replace the town and buildings, a total of 23,000 hectares of forest was destroyed. The fire also shut down pipelines, reducing the amounts of oil and gas available for export.

Alberta had 189 wildfires in 2011, all caused by human activities such as sparks from trains, construction or oil pipeline work, careless smoking, campfires or ATV exhaust pipes. Unfortunately, serious fires such as the Slave Lake fire are still likely in the future.

AIR CANADA FLIGHT 797

It was June 2, 1983, and Canadian folk singer Stan Rogers tried to stretch his long frame as best he could on the Air Canada DC-9 jet. He was grumpy and hated flying. He worried that baggage handlers would crush his precious twelve-string guitar as they had done a few years before. The red-bearded, bald-headed performer had just come from the Kerrville Folk Festival in Texas where he'd been the headline performer. This appearance in the United States was a big boost for his popularity and would lead to more recognition at home in Canada.

Air Canada flight 797 was flying at 10,000 metres, a routine trip between Dallas, Texas, Toronto and Montreal. Only forty-one passengers were on board, along with five crew members. Most were Canadians, returning home from business or holiday in the southern United States.

Halfway to Toronto, a flight attendant noticed smoke coming from one of the rear washrooms. Had someone tossed a cigarette into the waste bin? Using a fire extinguisher, he was unsuccessful in putting out the flames. Acrid smoke was curling out between the plastic panels. The pilots were told, and the co-pilot investigated. Suddenly a master warning light came on, and many electrical systems began to fail. The pilot, Captain Donald Cameron, was left with only basic instruments. He made an emergency call: "Mayday. Mayday. We are going down. We have a fire." The jet was given clearance to the nearest airport, in Cincinnati, Ohio.

Meanwhile, smoke began to fill the passenger cabin. The PA system shut down as well, so the flight attendants had to shout instructions to the passengers. They also showed people sitting next to emergency exits how to open the doors in order to evacuate the plane more quickly, something that is done today, but wasn't at the time. The pilot's navigation instruments failed, so ground control began giving the pilot instructions when to turn and descend. Within twelve minutes, the DC-9 was lined up with the runway. By now, chunks of melted plastic were falling from the ceiling. Passengers covered their mouths and moved closer to the front to avoid the dense smoke.

The smoke from the melted plastic contained cyanide and other toxins, as well as deadly carbon monoxide gas. Carbon monoxide poisoning causes people to become extremely sleepy, leading to unconsciousness and possibly death.

Smoke was also thick in the cockpit. The pilot could barely see his instruments, and he couldn't see the airport at all. When the passenger jet finally hit the runway, it came down hard, blowing all the tires.

The passengers were calm and quiet as they prepared to exit. As soon as the plane stopped, three of the emergency doors were opened and people began climbing onto the wings. The smoke was so thick in the aircraft, some passengers turned the wrong way and missed the exits. In the front of the aircraft, the co-pilot climbed out the cockpit emergency exit window and fell five metres to the ground, but the pilot was disoriented and remained in his seat. Only when firefighters sprayed him with foam did he revive enough to climb out the window.

Just ninety seconds after evacuation, a flash-fire ripped through the jet. The incoming fresh air had fully ignited the smouldering fire. Twenty-three passengers were trapped inside. All were killed.

Investigators found many of the dead still strapped to their seats, making it likely they were unconscious as the plane rolled to a stop. Tests showed high levels of toxins in their blood. Among the dead was Stan Rogers.

Stories were circulated later of a large bald man with a red beard who helped others get out of the aircraft. The stories got more dramatic with each telling. But what is known for sure is that Canada lost a gifted folk singer and songwriter.

Investigators discovered the fire was electrical but could not trace it to an exact location. Investigators, pilots and passenger groups across North America insisted on long-overdue changes to aircraft safety.

Within five years, aircraft manufacturers had installed smoke detectors and automatic fire extinguishers on all passenger aircraft. Seat cushions were made with fire-suppressing material and all aircraft would have lighting in the aisles to allow passengers to exit in smoky conditions. Although there have been improvements to modern aircraft, deadly fires can still occur.

QUEBEC CITY FIRE OF 1845

Quebec City is a beautiful place and the oldest section, Vieux Quebec, is a popular tourist destination. Visitors from across the country and from many nations enjoy the European flavour of the city. But Quebec didn't always look this way.

After a few days of hot weather, on May 28, 1845, a fire began at a tannery in the neighbourhood of St. Roch. A vat of flammable dye had broken open over a fire. Flames consumed the tannery building and a poorly organized effort to put out the fire, made worse by strong winds, allowed the fire to spread. Sheds and barns, piles of hay in the streets and stacks of firewood in every yard fed the flames. Church bells rang the alarm and many people escaped with just the clothes on their back. Street after street of densely packed wooden houses were destroyed in minutes. Flames leaped from roof to roof. The fire had consumed nearly half of the lower town when, at the request of the mayor, soldiers set explosive charges inside a row of houses in the path of the fire. Homeowners were given little time to escape with their children, their animals and a few bits of furniture before their houses were flattened by exploding gunpowder. The collapsed houses prevented the fire from advancing further, saving the rest of the lower town. The fire killed dozens of people and left thousands homeless. Fifteen hundred houses and 3,000 buildings were destroyed.

On June 28, exactly one month later, a second fire struck the lower town, this time ravaging the remaining St. Jean Baptiste section. These crowded dwellings housed regular inhabitants plus people who had fled the earlier fire. This fire began when someone accidently dumped cinders onto a manure pile. Again, a stiff wind blew the flames across the remaining section of the lower town, destroying 1,300 houses and buildings and leaving thousands homeless. Two fires had now destroyed almost the entire lower town, about two-thirds of the city. Only the upper town remained unburned.

Before rebuilding efforts began, the mayor insisted on strict guidelines to prevent another fire. Besides enforcing long-standing rules about not leaving heaps of straw and manure piles littering the streets, homeowners were told not to stack firewood against buildings and were limited to how much gunpowder they could store in their house. More importantly, homeowners were forced to build safer houses. Each new house was to have a thick stone wall separating it from the next building. These stone walls were to extend above the roof level. Ladders were to be put on all roofs to improve access in case of a fire. Shingles could not be made of wood, but had to be slate or tin. As a result of these changes, there have been no more devastating fires, and the magnificent stone houses still stand proudly in old Quebec.

THE VANCOUVER FIRE

Fur traders and gold miners were some of the first Europeans to head overland to Canada's west coast. After they moved on, lumber mills moved in. Sawmills appeared on nearly every river. When the small town of Granville, nicknamed

The makeshift city hall after the fire.

"Gastown," was chosen for the last stop on the Canadian Pacific Railroad, it became the place we now call Vancouver. The town spread like a wild thing, advancing over hillsides and up the mountain slopes. Forests were stripped of timber, and leftover branches and stumps, called slash, lay drying in heaps beside every road and clearing.

On June 13, a burning pile of slash north of the city flared out of control and a steady wind blew the fire southward. People saw the approaching fire and began to run, later recalling they had no time even to lace up a pair of boots. Most people ran for Burrard Inlet. Some were trapped by the flames and died. Witnesses described how a house would "blister on the bare boards and shimmer a moment or two with the heat waves. Then the whole outside of the building would be a mass of white flame." In one part of town, people huddled in a ditch while others a few metres away burned to death. Some hid in shallow wells only to be suffocated as the flames passing above them removed the oxygen from the air. Those who fled into Burrard Inlet went out into the water using logs to help them float. After a few hours the fire burned itself out.

It was amazing how quickly the townspeople rebuilt the city. Tents served to replace stores and the city hall. Cities that usually competed with Vancouver helped out. New Westminster sent lumber and $9,000, which was a lot of money in those days. Within twelve hours rebuilding had begun. Vancouver soon was bigger than ever before and it has been growing ever since.

THE TORONTO FIRE

Like many cities, Toronto grew rapidly in the early 1900s as more and more immigrants settled in the New World. By 1904, Toronto's wooden buildings were quickly replaced by structures with beautiful stone fronts. Toronto had its own Flatiron building, like the famous one in New York. This triangle-shaped building stood an impressive five stories high. Timothy Eaton had a new store with escalators that entertained Toronto children for hours on end. City Hall was an imposing stone building, and the steeple on St. James Cathedral was the tallest in North America.

Unfortunately, Toronto's growth was too fast, and safety standards had not been maintained. On the night of April 19, 1904, a fire began at the E&S Currie building on Wellington Street West. Firemen quickly arrived after a night watchman reported the fire, but poor water pressure and outdated equipment made it difficult for them to battle the fire. Strong winds fanned the flames and the fire got much worse. In the dead of night, the blaze spread to many nearby buildings.

The remains of downtown Toronto after the fire.

Most had stone fronts but were primarily made of wood inside. One after another, they were consumed by the blaze. Toronto fire crews were unable to stop the fire, and an emergency train was sent out to bring experienced firefighters from as far away as Hamilton and Buffalo, New York. They arrived in time to help stop the eastward spread of the fire at Yonge Street.

In the end, the fire did $10 million damage to the city. Eighty hectares of its core, totalling ninety-eight buildings and one hundred and thirty-seven businesses, were completely destroyed. For days, a smouldering ruin was all that was left of one of the busiest areas of the city.

Unlike major fires in many cities, and luckily for Toronto, there was not one fatality in Toronto's Great Fire of 1904.

WHEN THE EARTH BREAKS

THE DEADLY CROWSNEST PASS

The Crowsnest Pass winds through Canada's Rocky Mountains and is one of the most beautiful places in Canada. This one-hundred-kilometre route straddles the border between British Columbia and Alberta, meanders between gentle slopes and tree-lined valleys, pristine lakes and the sharp peaks of the Rocky Mountains. But the beauty is misleading. No other region of Canada has such a deadly history.

Below the towering mountains lie the graves of more than 600 people who died from fire, explosion, rockslides, avalanches or disease. The stories of the Crowsnest Pass are about those who lost their lives building the railway.

FERNIE FIRES OF CROWSNEST PASS

Some local legends claim that the problems visited on the people in Crowsnest Pass are the result of a curse. According to legend, a chief of the Kootenay tribe put a curse of "death, fire, hunger and misery" on the area because William Fernie, who bought the land, insulted the

chief's daughter. The story says that Fernie was more inter-
ested in the "black gold" necklace the chief's daughter wore
(it was made of coal) than in the girl herself. Though the
legend is likely fiction, some people wonder . . .

In 1900, the town of Fernie was only two years old.
Typical of towns in the Crowsnest Pass, it had sprung from
the dense forest to become a town of 2,000 in two short years
since the railroad came through. This was no workman's
camp. This was a complete town with streets, businesses,
stores, churches, a skating rink, sports fields and several
hotels. There was enough money here that the town even
had modern conveniences such as electric lights. In another
year, the population rose to 3,000 people, making Fernie the
third-largest town in the British Columbia interior.

But there were growing pains. In 1904, the first of a
series of fires, caused by a brushfire, wiped out the entire
downtown area of stores and businesses. Within days, the
rebuilding began and town council enacted laws which
were supposed to prevent fires from doing such damage
again. The laws didn't work. In 1905, another fire broke out,
destroying several rows of buildings. Exactly a year later, a
fire in a tailor shop destroyed most of the rebuilt buildings in
the hotel block. Surprisingly, fire control and safe practices
were still not in place when Fernie had its worst fire in 1908.

On August 1, a collapse of layers of rock and coal, called
a "bump," trapped twenty-eight miners in the nearby Coal
Creek Mine, which kept people's attention focused on the

mine site. Nobody was watching a small but persistent fire in a pile of slash beside a lumber company yard. In the early hours of the morning the wind fanned the flames that spread to stacked and dried lumber. Sparks from this blaze carried to downtown Fernie and the fire spread with incredible swiftness. Eyewitnesses claimed that a man on a horse could not have outrun the flames. Many people left town as the towering columns of smoke advanced. Others took refuge in a large stone office of the Coal Company and a warehouse where men doused the roof with water.

Fifteen hundred people were loaded onto thirty boxcars of a passing train and were taken to safety. Others crossed the Elk River. In an hour and a half, the town was almost completely destroyed. Gone were the new brewery, all the hotels, and the Canadian Pacific Railway's (CPR) station, freight shed, passenger and freight cars and coal chutes. The CPR train tracks were left twisted. Every store was left in ashes, as were the two newspaper offices and all but twenty-three homes. Almost six thousand people were left homeless. Remarkably, only ten people died in the fire, including a family who had hidden in a well as the fire passed over them.

Neighbouring communities of Cranbrook and Spokane, Washington, contributed tents, food and other provisions. An entire printing press was sent for free from Winnipeg, leaving the *Fernie Free Press* with a printed newspaper just days after the fire.

Fernie was eventually rebuilt with stone and other

fireproof materials. While smaller Crowsnest Pass towns disappeared over the years, Fernie grew larger. When coal became less important to the world, even Fernie almost disappeared. But demand for coal returned in the 1980s and Fernie is still thriving today.

THE NIGHT THE MOUNTAIN FELL

In 1903, the town of Frank, Alberta, was a noisy mining community of six hundred people. One of the newest mining towns of the Crowsnest Pass area, Frank had been built just three years earlier but already had an electric generating station, a school, four hotels, two doctors, a dentist and sixteen other businesses. Dominion Avenue was like something out of a wild west movie — a dirt street with wooden sidewalks. Identical wood-frame homes were spaced out in the northwest part of town, occupied by miners with families. Other houses were rented by groups of single miners. Numerous tents dotted the fields, housing labourers who were mostly drifters, known only by nicknames. These men worked a few months, got paid in cash, and drifted on. Nobody knew how many there were.

The town of Frank was built directly beneath Turtle Mountain, which loomed 1,000 metres high above the town. Residents of Frank enjoyed the view, but local Kootenay people would never camp there. They claimed the mountain moved slowly, like a turtle, and one day the turtle would nod his head and roll down the mountain. To the townsfolk, such notions were ridiculous.

The mine in Turtle Mountain was very productive, filling rail cars with hundreds of tonnes of coal daily. With hardly a swing of a pickaxe, coal would fall out of thick seams that ran inside the mountain.

On April 29, nineteen miners entered the mine at midnight to install support timbers and repair track. In the town below, most of the day-shift miners were sleeping or enjoying a final drink at one of the hotels. Over the prior weeks, some miners had noticed that some of the ground had shifted; there had also been tremors. There were other strange things: gaps where coal had been extracted were found tightly slammed together a few hours later; timbers recently set in place were found to have suddenly shifted. But that night, all was quiet. The men worked in crews of three or four and then stopped for their lunch break at 4 a.m. Alfred Clark, Fred Farrington and Alexander Tashigan stood in the fresh air of the mine entrance to eat their lunches beside the mine tipple, where coal was dumped into rail cars. They chose the wrong place to eat their lunch.

At 4:10 a.m., the top section of Turtle Mountain, almost a kilometre wide and weighing about 80 million tons, broke loose and began to slide, burying the three miners. As it fell, the mountainside broke into boulders the size of houses and buses, which skipped and bounced onto the sleeping town below, crushing and pulverizing everything in their path. Every home and building in the northwest section of Frank was flattened like paper and buried fifteen metres deep under the rubble. On and on the boulders surged, filling the valley floor and rolling halfway up the slope on the opposite side, covering the Oldman River, Gold Creek, the CPR tracks, the mine entrance, the power plant, many houses and a train boxcar filled with dynamite. In about ninety seconds, almost one hundred people, together with their homes, were buried beneath tons of broken rock.

This view of Turtle Mountain shows the path of the mountain's collapse.

In the main part of town, just beside where the mountain fell, houses shook and a blast of wind pounded windows and doors. The roar of the mountain's collapse was deafening. Townsfolk with lanterns set out to see if the mine had collapsed. They were stunned to find a field of boulders as far as the eye could see. A few boards and shingles lay scattered over the rocks, all that remained of houses buried deep below. Twenty-three survivors were eventually pulled from the wreckage of their homes, but only twelve bodies were recovered. Most of the dead lay buried too deep to be reached.

At the edge of destruction, one half of a house may have been pulverized and the other half left standing. In the Leitch home, Jessie and May Leitch were found alive, pinned on their bed beneath a ceiling joist, but their four brothers and parents were dead. The most miraculous survivor was the youngest daughter: Marion Leitch was just a baby in her crib when the boulders hit the house. She was thrown out of the house and into the air, landing softly on a pile of hay which had flown out of the collapsed stable next door.

Canadian Pacific Railway brakeman Sid Choquette became the hero of songs and stories. His train, which had just picked up coal cars from the mine, barely escaped being crushed by the falling mountain. Sid knew that a passenger train, the *Spokane Flyer*, was due any moment and would crash into the boulders laying over the track. Choquette clambered over the broken boulders to warn the train engineer. He flagged the train down just in time, preventing it from slamming into the Frank Slide.

Deep inside the mountain, the other miners felt and heard the terrible shaking; they were certain one of their tunnels had collapsed. Finding the main entryway blocked, they began to dig their way out, but soon the water of the Oldman River began to fill the lower levels. Without air coming in, poisonous gases leaking from the coal deposit started to gather. The miners climbed to a higher level, they remembered a coal seam that led to the outside of the mountain. After thirteen hours of back-breaking work, the miners succeeded in digging themselves out through a narrow gap, while just a few metres below them, off-duty miners were working to get to them from the outside. Seventeen men climbed out of the mine, among them Charles Elick and William Warrington. Warrington, one of the last out, stared, disbelieving, at the layer of broken boulders that now covered the entire valley. His joy at being safe turned to sorrow when he saw that rocks covered what had been his home with his wife and daughters inside. The exact number of those killed in the slide is unknown. But between sixty-nine and seventy-six people were likely buried by Turtle Mountain.

Geologists who studied the land concluded that the Frank Slide was caused by diagonal fault lines, or cracks, in the mountain, that had widened over time. A few days before the slide, the weather was hot. On the day of the slide, the temperature had dropped to below freezing. Water may have entered the fault lines and frozen, expanding the cracks and overcoming the balance the mountain had achieved over the years. Mining of the coal seams certainly helped make it unstable. The study concluded that the mountain was destined to fall.

Perhaps the Kootenay were right; the turtle had nodded its head.

CANADA'S WORST MINE DISASTER: THE HILLCREST MINE

Mining was the major source of wealth in the Crowsnest Pass. The rich coal deposits provided a ready source of fuel for train engines and home heating. Mining was regular employment for hundreds of men and paid an average wage of $120 a month. This allowed them a lifestyle they could never have had elsewhere. Workers came from across Europe, including England, Italy, Scotland, Ukraine, Germany, Ireland and Poland.

In 1914, halfway up a slope of land facing Frank, Alberta, was the little town of Hillcrest and the Hillcrest Mine. Seeing the boulders of the Frank Slide every day, knowing about the seventy or more people buried underneath them, should have made the miners uneasy. But the Hillcrest Mine had a good safety record. It had gone nine years without a major problem.

Hillcrest had all the typical dangers of a coal mine. The explosive methane gas usually found with coal deposits was present, but the Hillcrest mine had powerful ventilation fans and barriers that brought clean air into the mine and vented the methane out. Coal dust can also explode if it is allowed to build up in the mine, but the men removed it regularly and dampened dusty areas with water. Since it took a single spark to ignite methane or coal dust, all equipment was carefully designed not to give off sparks. Blasting out coal with explosives was only done by an explosives expert, called a "fire boss."

Even if a mine disaster were to happen at Hillcrest, the miners were ready. Special rescue teams practised using mine-rescue equipment provided by the governments of Alberta and British Columbia.

On June 19, 1914, the mine had been inspected during the night shift. There were small pockets of methane here and there and a few minor rock falls. The superintendent entered the mine early with a crew to vent the gas. Later that morning, 235 men entered the gloomy drifts and slopes and descended to their various work places. Around 9:30 a.m., men were doing routine tasks: Thomas Bardsley took a swing with his heavy pickaxe at a coal face off Level 1. Charles Ironmonger was hauling cars of coal to the upper mine entrance. Below him at the Number 2 entrance, another young man, Fred Kurigatz was doing the same thing with other coal cars.

Then, somewhere on Level 1 South, a spark ignited a pocket of methane gas. In a moment, the explosion travelled hundreds of metres through tunnels and slopes, igniting other pockets of methane and coal dust. The explosive fire used up most of the life-giving oxygen in the mine. Those near the blast, in Tunnels 31 to 35, were thrown into the nearest wall and died instantly. Some were killed by the violent concussion of the blast itself. Men farther away were knocked flat, their lamps blown away or clothing torn open. The sound of the blast, like that of a cannon, came a second after.

Bodies would later be found frozen into their last action, holding tools in a death grip, their eyes staring. Charles Ironmonger was hurled twenty metres from inside the mine to the hoist house on surface. He died soon after. Fred Kurigatz was killed after he was thrown against a wall just inside the mine entry. Thomas Bardsley died gripping his pickaxe.

Those who were still conscious began a desperate struggle to leave the mine. Most knew that deadly afterdamp, poisonous gases mixed with carbon monoxide, would be almost everywhere. Afterdamp would kill in minutes if someone stumbled into it. If the men stayed where they were, the afterdamp might find them first.

A pillar of brown smoke rose from both the entrances to the mine, and the townsfolk gathered. Off-duty miners began to arrive. The mine manager sent for mine rescue units with breathing apparatus, and the ventilation fans were repaired to force fresh air into the mine.

In the mine, some survivors stumbled in darkness

because their safety lamps had been broken. Dizzy from lack of oxygen and deaf from the blast, many stumbled into afterdamp, fell into unconsciousness and died.

Of the 235 men who entered the mine that morning, only eighteen were able to escape the mine on their own, staggering out of the entrance in ones and twos, retching and coughing the filthy gases from their lungs. David Murray made it out, but not finding his three sons, turned back toward the deadly tunnels. A policeman tried to stop him, but couldn't. Later, Murray was found, killed by afterdamp. Charles Elick, who had survived the Frank Slide, was found dead. Rescuers found survivors and whisked them to the surface in a mine car. They also found a group of about thirty miners drowned in a shallow pool of water. In total, just forty men escaped the mine. One hundred eighty-nine had died. Hillcrest was the worst Canadian mine disaster in history.

Three North West Mounted Police corporals were assigned to investigate the deaths and keep order. From years of being on opposite sides of bar fights and picket lines, Mounties and miners had no love for each other. But respect for the Mounties grew when miners saw them spend days at the gruesome task of sorting out bodies of dead miners for burial. In turn, Mounties began to appreciate the miners, who led them safely through the labyrinth of ruined mine tunnels to recover the dead.

Multiple tragedies struck many families. Three Dugdale

brothers were working the same shift but only one came out of the mine alive. Jonathan Penn, a schoolboy, saw the brown smoke rising above the mine and ran to the mine site. He would lose both his father and brother to the mine. Rod Wallis and William Neath, brothers-in-law, were due to return to Nova Scotia the following week, but neither of them would make that journey.

In any city or town, losing 189 men would be a terrible tragedy. But to a tiny community like Hillcrest, it was devastating. Nearly every family in town was missing at least one member. One hundred and thirty wives suddenly became widows, and about 400 children were left fatherless. Across the young province of Alberta, people and businesses donated money to support the widows. The company provided $1,800 to each family, which was a generous amount of money in those days. The federal government gave $50,000 and the provincial government $20,000 to divide among the families. Most of the dead were buried in three mass graves below Turtle Mountain.

Investigators believed that the explosion was set off by a spark, perhaps from a pickaxe, machinery or a falling rock striking other rocks.

Surprisingly, the Hillcrest Mine was soon up and running. In 1926, there was another explosion that killed two men working the midnight shift. Had the explosion happened just a few hours later, 150 men might have died. Eventually, as more people switched to oil instead of coal as heating fuel, the Hillcrest Mine closed. In 1949, the site of Canada's worst mine disaster was sealed with a dynamite blast, leaving the tunnels and slopes in darkness forever.

THE DEADLY COAL CREEK MINE

On May 22, 1902, 200 men were working the afternoon-to-midnight shift in the Coal Creek Mine near Fernie. Just after 7:30 p.m., a massive explosion rocked the mine, blowing apart the ventilation shed and sending smoke and flames 300 metres into the air. The explosion destroyed the ventilation system leading into the mine, which meant rescuers couldn't enter. Dozens of men worked to restore the pipes. They had no special breathing equipment, so each man worked until he fainted from lack of oxygen. He would be carried out and replaced by someone else. Rescuers worked hours until they could re-enter the mine. All ninety men working the Number 2 mine were already dead. Thirty-eight were killed in the Number 3 mine; only twenty were rescued. There were so many dead that coffins were in short supply and had to be shipped by trainloads from neighbouring towns. Mass funerals were held every hour. Some of the miners' bodies were so badly mutilated they were taken directly from the mine to the graveyard.

It was Canada's second worst mine disaster. The lives of one hundred and twenty-eight men were snuffed out.

Despite the terrible loss of life, the Coal Creek Mine soon reopened. It was a rich mine and had many varieties of coal.

On July 31, 1908, a collapse of layers of rock and coal called a "bump" killed three miners and trapped twenty other men for eight hours. The Number 2 mine was closed shortly afterward. In December 1912, a slide of rock and snow crashed onto the Coal Creek Mine destroying various buildings above the ground and killing six men. In 1917, another explosion took the lives of thirty-four men in the mine, and in 1928 another six died. In 1935, another major bump took three lives. By 1958, the Coal Creek Mine was closed for good, ending sixty years of employment in coal production, but costing over 190 lives.

EAST COAST MINE DISASTERS

Springhill, Nova Scotia, has long been associated with mine disasters and dramatic rescue. The layers of coal began to be mined in the 1850s, and mining has become a permanent part of the area's history. These Springhill stories tell of disaster, uncommon bravery and perseverance. But the more recent Westray Mine tragedy makes us wonder if we have learned anything from the last 150 years of fatalities in coal mining.

THE SPRINGHILL MINE EXPLOSION OF 1891

Fourteen-year-old Bruce Ryan's mining clothes were stiff with coal dust as he began the long walk to the Number 2 coal mine in Springhill, Nova Scotia. His muscles still ached from yesterday's long shift of shovelling coal. Bruce had no choice but to work: his father had been killed in the mine, and he now supported his mother and two young brothers. Bruce watched other boys and girls his age walking to school, wearing clean clothes and carrying books. He sometimes bragged to them about doing a "man's job," but secretly he envied them.

Ryan never admitted that he was afraid of the mine. Older miners casually talked about "bumps," when whole sections of the mine would collapse, or coal dust explosions which could kill a hundred men in a few seconds of burning terror . . . but they always happened in other mines. The men believed the Springhill mines to be among the safest in Nova Scotia. But Ryan didn't feel safe in the Number 2 mine. Not today and not ever. He wished there was some other job he could do.

It was just after lunch on February 21, 1891, when an explosion ripped through the narrow passages of the mine. The blast carried on through the Number 1 and Number 2 mine, doing less damage as the distance increased but still blowing out miners' lamps and causing confusion through-out the many kilometres of the mine.

The shockwave tore through the east side; an eruption of white flame burned nearby men, boys and pit ponies. The shock pushed timbers from their places, and unstable areas of coal collapsed. Equipment was scattered was destroyed. Shouts sounded in the darkness as dazed survivors scrambled to locate their partners or find their way to the surface. Dozens of men were killed when, stumbling through the darkness, they came upon the deadly afterdamp.

Younger boys like Joseph Dupee, John Dunn and Willard Carter, only twelve and thirteen years old, died in the mine. Fathers and grandfathers, boys and men . . . in all, one hundred and twenty-five died. The Springhill Mine Explosion of 1891 remains one of the worst mine disasters in Canada.

And yet, in all the misery and death there was heroism. Hundreds of off-duty miners ignored the danger, put on their equipment and ran to the mine. They cautiously entered the crumbling, gas-filled tunnels to search for survivors. Many lives were saved by those who, swallowing their fears, returned to the passageways again and again. Half-dead survivors, those who had been blinded or crippled by rock falls, were hauled out even as timber and falling coal threatened their lives. Danny Robertson, a fourteen-year-old who suffered serious burns to his back, hands and face, somehow managed to carry another boy, Willie Terris, out of the mine on his back. Store owner John Wilson, an ex-miner, entered the mine in his business suit and for twenty-four hours helped search the familiar old tunnels for signs of life. Jessie Armishaw left the mine in shock when he found the bodies of three of his sons huddled together in death.

People from around the world, including Queen Victoria and Governor General Lord Arthur Stanley, sent their condolences.

But in years to come, Springhill would face even more tragedy.

THE SPRINGHILL MIRACLE OF 1956

The Springhill Mine was repaired and reopened. Over the years, the work conditions improved, although lung disease from breathing coal dust and fatal accidents were still far too common among miners. At least Canada's child labour laws ensured boys would no longer work underground. Springhill's rich coal deposits continued to supply coal for furnaces and factories all over Canada.

Parts of the Springhill mine were so deep it took men more than an hour to get to where they mined the coal. On November 1, 1956, at the Number 4 mine, a train of cars filled with coal dust was being pulled to the surface. The dust was being removed for safety, but as the train passed ventilation fans, a lot of it was blown back into the air. Then, near the surface, several train cars broke free. They sped back down until they derailed, more than a kilometre into the mine. One of the cars cut a 2,500-volt electrical cable and the shower of sparks triggered a massive explosion. Walls of flame scorched through many tunnels, killing thirty-two miners below ground and seven men on the surface. Eighty-eight men were trapped deep in the lower levels; nobody knew if there were any survivors.

Mine rescuers hurried in to help. Some were "draegermen," carrying thirty-five–kilogram fresh-air draeger tanks on their backs; others were "barefaced" men, who had no extra breathing equipment. At any moment, loose layers of rock, timber or wooden platforms could fall. Pockets of poisonous afterdamp lurked in low areas. Nevertheless, the search continued for days. Deep in the mine, the eighty-eight trapped miners prayed for a miracle. After three-and-a-half days, just when people were beginning to lose hope, the trapped men were found and rescued. The survivors became known as the Springhill Miracle.

THE SPRINGHILL MIRACLE OF 1958

Springhill's last and most famous disaster happened in 1958. The Number 2 mine at Springhill was the largest in North America. Some of its longer tunnels extended three kilometres into the earth, well beneath the Atlantic Ocean. Hundreds of kilometres of other passages crisscrossed through the coal layer. The layers of shale and sandstone bedrock above the coal were supported by heavy wood beams, pillars of rock and platforms.

A weary rescue worker is covered in coal dust after searching for survivors.

On October 23, at 8:06 p.m., a massive collapse of the layers of bedrock, a "bump," flattened large sections of the mine. It was the strongest mine bump ever recorded in North America. The shockwave was felt hundreds of kilometres away; scientists believed it was an earthquake. Within the first few moments, seventy-four miners were killed when the rock above their heads collapsed on them. Nearly one hundred other miners were trapped in deeper sections, but nobody knew if they had survived. Off-duty miners and rescue workers raced to Springhill. Dozens of draegermen descended into the wrecked tunnels, crawling under groaning timbers, shining their lamps into every crevice that may have hidden a body. Seventy-five men were found almost at the bottom of the mine, walking and helping the injured toward the surface. All around them, many sections of the mine were inaccessible, but the draegermen continued to search for the living and remove bodies of the dead. Days passed and many men were still missing, increasing the agony for families waiting on the surface.

Reporters from all over the world waited with the families at the Number 2 mine. Would there be another Springhill miracle? Canadians watched the drama unfold in their living rooms as CBC camera crews broadcast the event live from Springhill, a rare thing in those days.

After five days, hope began to die out. Some mine officials feared for the safety of the searchers and felt the rescue efforts should end. The draegermen insisted on continuing. Incredibly, six-and-a-half days after the bump, twelve desperate men were found in a space so small they could only lie flat. Maurice Ruddick, who had been singing for days to help them keep their hopes up, shouted into a pipe just as rescuers passed the other end of it, dozens of metres away. Two days later, seven more men were found, trapped but alive, their spirits helped along, again, by singing. Finally, one more man was found in a space no larger than a grave, an incredible nine days after the disaster.

Following the 1958 tragedy, the Springhill mines were closed. The people of Springhill had seen enough death and disaster.

THE WESTRAY MINE DISASTER

Trevor Jahn and Ferris Dewan were quiet as they rode underground for a long twelve-hour shift in the Westray coal mine. They had been friends since elementary school and had worked in various mines together from one end of the country to the other. They were good miners and usually enjoyed the work. But now both men were nervous. This new and modern mine was the most dangerous place they had ever worked in. Rock falls were so common that the men had stopped counting the number of times they had jumped out of the way to avoid being hit by falling slabs of coal. Explosive methane gas was found in high levels in many parts of the mine. All coal mines produce some of this poisonous and explosive gas, but proper fresh air ventilation systems continually remove methane and keep it well below danger levels. At Westray, the ventilation system wasn't working properly. Increasing the danger of explosions, coal dust, which can burn quickly or explode, was building up in work areas.

Both Jahn and Dewan knew how a coal mine should be operated. Coal mines can be made reasonably safe, but this wasn't being done at Westray. Not only was there too much explosive and flammable material around, but the men were being given equipment to use which could give off sparks — which is strictly against the law in coal mines. One miner recalled seeing a mechanic remove a methane safety switch from a digging machine. This safety device would shut the machine down if it detected high levels of methane. "It runs better without it," was the mechanic's reply when the miner objected.

There weren't many jobs at the time, so the men should have been happy to find steady work, but Jahn had had enough. He was saving enough money to leave this mine; he was about two weeks short of his goal.

Miles Gillis, another miner with many years' experience, was certain there would be an explosion. He feared for his life. He was so certain that an explosion would occur, he had shown a friend a map of the mine, pointing out the southwest section, saying that was where the blast would happen. He also predicted that all the men working in that area would be killed. Though he tried to hide his fears from his wife at first, in time he told her how afraid he was. With tears in his eyes, he made his wife promise to call for an investigation into the mine if the blast happened while he was underground.

Miners can't afford to be nervous people. But these experienced men believed an explosion or a major cave-in would happen sooner or later. Many of them reported the unsafe conditions to the mine managers and the government, but nothing much was done. The mine was the only steady work many of them had had in years.

In the early morning hours of May 9, 1992, a spark from one of the mining machines ignited the methane gas. The sudden flash of fire sent a fatal shockwave and a wall of flame ripping through the mine. All twenty-six men who were in the mine that night were killed. After the flame died down, the wreckage-filled mine tunnels were silent and dark.

Gillis's prediction was correct: the blast began at the southwest section of the mine, and all the men there, including himself, were killed. Jahn and Dewan, friends in life, were also together in death.

Shaun Comish was one of the lucky ones. He was working the day shift and had left the mine just hours before the blast. Comish came back to the mine the next day, but this time as a draegerman, a rescue miner, to look for possible survivors. He described it this way: "I could not believe my eyes as we walked down into what can only be called hell … There was a smell I can't really describe, a smell of burning, mixed with the smell of pulverized rock … The further down we went, the worse it looked. Cement bulkheads that had been two to three metres thick had been smashed into little pieces and thrown a hundred feet or more. Steel doors that had been fifteen feet high and twelve feet wide were now crumpled, twisted pieces of strange-looking metal. Two transformers had been smashed together so hard they looked like one hunk of debris. The transformers, which weigh roughly three tonnes each, had been thrown about a hundred feet across the crosscut (tunnel) and down the decline . . ."

The next day Comish returned with other draegermen. By now, few people believed they would find any of the twenty-six men alive.

"Ahead we saw a fall of rock that went higher than the roof. It was impossible to go on. Just as we turned to go back we heard the rumble of another rock fall. Tonnes of rock were falling somewhere in the darkness. This scared us completely . . . We all thought the same thing. Were we trapped in? . . . Luckily as we climbed up piles of rocks we found our way had not been blocked."

Only fifteen of the twenty-six bodies were recovered from the mine.

The families of the dead men and the off-duty miners demanded an inquiry. It became the most important cause in their lives to see that their friends and relatives not be buried and forgotten with the mine. The fear that another Westray could happen again had driven them on.

A detailed study by Justice K. Peter Richard blamed the mine managers. So many violations of safe mining practice were found that he concluded the explosion was certain to happen, the only question was when? He titled his report: "The Westray Story: A Predictable Path to Disaster."

Justice Richard also blamed the Government of Nova

Scotia's Department of Natural Resources and Department of Labour for the disaster. If they had been strict in enforcing the rules, the mine management would have been forced to change or shut down.

One can only hope that the shame this tragedy brings will prevent another mine disaster like Westray from happening again.

NATURE'S FURY

A country as large as Canada sees a huge variety of weather. Deadly floods may hit Manitoba, while the east coast may be unusually dry. Canadian ice storms are well known, but British Columbia seldom gets snow. Hurricanes may ravage the Atlantic Provinces but seldom reach Quebec or Ontario. Tornadoes have always been more common in western Canada than in the rest of the country, but now affect the Great Lakes region. It is important that we all remember past weather events and learn to always be prepared.

THE HURRICANE OF 1775: CANADA'S DEADLIEST

Climate change is blamed for recent weather extremes, but we also had killer storms hundreds of years ago. The worst hurricane in Canadian history hit Newfoundland from September 10 to 12, 1775, killing 4,000 people, most of them drowning at sea.

The Newfoundland cod fishery of the 1700s was mostly done by European fishermen who came during the summer and returned home every winter. It was a dangerous business. Few of them ever learned to swim in the cold ocean, and if they fell overboard, they were often as good as dead. The frequent storms could smash a precious fishing boat into shore, so when a storm came, skippers sailed their boats away from the rocky coastline. But by doing this they also risked capsizing and drowning. Many fishermen died at sea.

Every summer, the men and boys lived in shacks that dotted Newfoundland's rocky shoreline. While the older men fished, young apprentices gutted, split, salted and dried the codfish. When the winds picked up, the younger ones looked to sea and wondered if their brothers or fathers would return.

The autumn of 1775 brought unusually calm water and poor catches. On September 10, those conditions lured the fishermen out into their boats. But things quickly changed. One person recalled: "Over the horizon to the southeast there spread an orange hued glow. Then wisps of wind, that slowly gathered strength and increasing . . . culminated in the fierce violence of hurricane . . . hatches were battened, boats lashed and sails double reefed. Ships slipped their chains and strove to escape . . . Only one small schooner, whose skipper had foreseen disaster, was able to round Salvage Point to the south and reach Ochre Pit Cove to ride out the storm. The others were driven to death."

Another eyewitness recalled: "One apprentice lad lived

through the horrors of that awful night. The tide had risen full 20 feet above its normal level, and on the crest of a huge wave the boat with the boy lashed to the helm was carried up the sands and wedged between large trees . . ."

Waves rose to unheard of heights and tossed the vessels over like the bits of wood they were. Small fishing boats and large navy vessels were equal victims of the storm. Most of those who died were sailors and fishermen. The sea surge of hurricane-driven waves pounded the shoreline and destroyed fishermen's huts and storage sheds, killing some who were finding shelter. Small coastal villages reported docks torn loose, barns and storehouses destroyed and entire ships' cargoes lost.

The hurricane littered salted cod over vast stretches of shoreline. Spoiled cod floated in great islands of bobbing white patches, joined with the bodies of sailors. Survivors would always remember the tremendous stench.

For months, corpses were pulled from the ocean tangled in fishnets. Years later, human bones would still get washed up on beaches.

EDMONTON'S BLACK FRIDAY

It was sweltering hot in Edmonton at the end of July 1987. On Friday, July 31, thunderclouds rolled across the big sky of the prairie, promising relief from the heat. Many people were looking forward to the coming weekend. Mary Grandish was getting ready for a camping trip, but she and many others would not make it out of Edmonton that weekend.

Tom Taylor was leaving his pharmacy south of Edmonton when he saw a long, thin funnel descend from one of the black storm clouds that scudded northward. Fascinated, he watched it touch a farmer's field and turn black as dirt entered its swirling funnel. It was a small tornado, perhaps only ten metres wide, but still dangerous. He phoned the weather office and gave the first warning.

The black storm cloud moved toward Beaumont, just outside of Edmonton. Here again the deadly funnel cloud touched down, but it was now as wide as a football field and much more destructive. It sounded like a dozen freight trains. For almost an hour, the tornado spun wickedly, carving a path of destruction. As it steadily moved northward, it left behind pieces of what it had lifted and twisted: bits of houses, trees, cars, even animals and people, all lying together. Within an hour, a winding, ruinous path forty kilometres long was left behind.

The area hardest hit was the Evergreen Trailer Park. Ninety-one of the six hundred trailer homes were ripped open or flipped and another hundred were badly damaged.

Four members of the Reimer family, a father and three children, were found dead in the rubble of their home.

Another woman hugged her one-month-old baby to protect her from the storm. The baby lived, but the mother

The tornado roars through Edmonton.

was killed by flying debris. Many people were injured as broken bits of trailers and furniture whipped around and smashed into them. Mark Ernewein and his wife returned from shopping to find their home completely ripped apart. Fifteen people lost their lives in the Evergreen Trailer Park. Authorities were amazed the death toll wasn't higher.

An industrial area called Refinery Row looked like a battle zone after the tornado ripped through it. Twelve workers died under collapsing steel factory roofs or under cars and trucks that were tossed around like toys. Sixty businesses were severely damaged or destroyed in a few violent minutes.

But there were also miracles. The tornado passed through the Clareview neighbourhood where Rod and

Mary Grandish lived. Mary recalls, "The tornado came from the south, beside our house, so I could not see it . . . it got very dark and the streetlights came on. Through the front window I noticed our travel trailer being pulled across the driveway. Then the neighbour's garden shed landed in our yard and I knew we were in trouble. There was a sound like a jet plane. I went to the back door and as I watched, our garage was lifted right off the foundations and then it folded up and turned sideways. It collapsed in a heap. Then the roof of the house caved in and I thought we were going to die. It was like your worst nightmare. When it ended I had to find my son. I got to where Cody's room was, but the room was gone. So was his crib. There was nothing left. I thought, 'My God, the tornado has taken my son.'"

The rain and wind lashed at Mary and a friend as they searched for three-and-a-half-month-old Cody. In what remained of the master bedroom she saw his little feet sticking out from under wreckage.

"I was so worried at first, because he was so quiet and he was bleeding. I could tell he was still alive, but I didn't know how badly hurt he was. I kissed him and prayed he would be okay." Cody had only minor injuries from his dangerous ride in the tornado.

Emergency response teams reacted immediately. Police kept order and volunteers transported victims to the hospital. Gas company workers closed gas lines and electricians shut down power to prevent explosions or fires.

Firefighters doused flames and searched for those who had been trapped. Hospital emergency wards treated hundreds of injured people. Even pets were rescued and cared for by animal control officers.

Amazingly, in the destruction of over three hundred homes and sixty factories, Edmonton residents respected people's property. Only one person was arrested for looting.

Tornadoes that deadly are rare, and the chances of a tornado of that size and destructive power hitting a major city are always very slim. Still, most cities and towns prepare for such emergencies, training hospital staff, firefighters, police and ambulance crews in case a disaster visits.

This disaster cost twenty-seven lives and injured three hundred people. Property damage, estimated at $330 million, was then the highest in Alberta history. Of Canadian tornadoes, only the Regina Cyclone of 1912, which killed twenty-eight people, was worse.

FLOOD OF THE CENTURY: THE RED RIVER FLOOD OF 1997

Knowing it was coming didn't make it much easier. In 1997, people in Manitoba knew months before it happened that they might have a "flood of the century."

Weather forecasters noted that 1996 brought much more rainfall than usual, which soaked into the soil until it could hold no more. Following that was a long, cold winter, freezing the ground like rock and covering it with heavy snowfalls. A monster blizzard had left an incredible forty-three centimetres of snow. Forecasters said a late spring and sudden snowmelt would bring record amounts of water flooding over the land.

The forecasters' worst predictions came true. The snow-melt began late and sudden warm winds melted all the snow at once. The flooded Red River hit Grand Forks, North Dakota, first. Just south of the Manitoba border, Grand Forks was built where the Red River widens. The American National Weather service had predicted the flood would rise to about fifteen metres, but the water rose to sixteen-and-a-half metres and overwhelmed the earthen dikes built to protect the city. Hourly updates on American news programs showed the water overflowing one dike after another, finally showing downtown Grand Forks under several metres of water. Adding to the ruin of the city, some of the downtown buildings were burning above the water line, destroying by fire what hadn't already been ruined by the dirty water below.

Manitoba residents watched TV uneasily, wondering if Winnipeg would be next. The floodwater would reach them in just a few days.

Winnipeggers have had many floods in the past. The area around the city is so flat that water spreads like cola on a countertop. In 1950, the Red River overflowed its banks and became a 1,000-square-kilometre lake that flooded tens of thousands of homes, causing millions of dollars of destruction. Since that flood, dikes — long banks of earth used to prevent flooding — were built beside the Red River, and a floodway — an emergency water channel — was dug to divert floodwater around Winnipeg. Outside the city's protective dikes, small towns and individual homes had permanent ring dikes circling them.

Engineers checked their calculations again to see how high the flood could go. One of them, Ron Richardson, discovered that one of the main dikes was twenty-two kilometres too short and three metres too low. If Winnipeg was to be protected from floodwaters, this dike had to be raised and lengthened . . . and they had only three days.

From all over the province, earth-moving equipment and operators were called to help. They worked around the clock, the dike lit at night by brilliant flares dropped by helicopters. Many of the heavy equipment operators didn't even stop to eat, working eighteen hours straight. The final layers of dirt and plastic sheeting were laid down just as the waters began to test the new dike.

Elsewhere, the dirty floodwater rose, encircling towns, farms, buildings and houses south of Winnipeg that were built on higher ground or protected by ring dikes. The police ordered people to evacuate, but many refused to leave.

"This is my home and I am the only one who can protect it," said one man.

Homes are surrounded by water.

Homeowners and farmers worked day and night, patrolling their dikes as the water crept higher, endlessly filling gaps with sandbags. In many heartbreaking cases, the water won anyway, leaving a precious home soaked with polluted river water.

Help came from ordinary people. Schoolchildren, office workers and senior citizens turned out to fill sandbags. They filled, lifted, carried and placed sandbags until their arms were numb and their backs were too stiff to bend. Soldiers from all parts of Canada were also sent to Winnipeg. Armed Forces mechanic Steven Dusa and his unit drove their armoured vehicles, called Cougars, from Ontario to Manitoba to help. Cougars can go on land and water which would obviously be useful. However, like everyone else, their job turned into sandbagging, which Dusa did for three-and-a-half weeks.

He recalled, "In eleven years with the armed forces I have never seen such friendly response from people. People brought racks of donuts from the local coffee shop ... People baked cookies and brought them out. Everywhere we went, people gave us things at half price because we were there to help them."

The dikes around Winnipeg held and stayed dry, but south of the city, a flooded area forty kilometres wide was called "the Red Sea." Aluminum boats and motorized rubber rafts carried sandbags to isolated houses, brought groceries or bottled water, or ferried people off flooded property.

Roads, fields and railway tracks all disappeared beneath the brown waves of silty water. Houses and barns stood surrounded by water. Below the water surface, wells were contaminated, and grain bins and silos became useless masses of waste. Ring dikes surrounding towns like Grand Point and Ste. Agathe, which had held back water for one hundred years, were overwhelmed. Hundreds of homes were flooded.

Once the peak flood levels passed and the waters began to recede, there was a noisy celebration by those whose homes survived. Then the cleanup began for those whose homes had been flooded. Strangers from all parts of Canada came to the rescue. Carpeting was torn out, drywall replaced and woodwork repaired or removed.

Pat and Dan Koets, youth leaders in a small Ontario church, helped organize volunteers. Pat describes their work: "The kids were great. With fundraising and donations, they helped earn about $5,000 to pay the gas and expenses to go to Manitoba. Along the way, hotels and restaurants would give discounts if they heard that we were going to help with the flood. We were part of a clean-up crew organized by the Mennonite church. They provided the food and a place to stay and sent us out on jobs. Dan would use a power washer to wash the basements with Javex and water, and the kids and I would scrub and sweep the water into the drains. You would see these beautiful homes belonging to seniors. They had put everything into them for their retirement and now they were such a mess."

Their son Chris recalled: "We were helping an old man in a small house and he had lost everything. He couldn't even afford food, so he was given meals by the Mennonites the same as we were ... The man cried. He had nothing left. Just before we left, my friend Mike and I drove out to his place and gave him the rest of the money we had saved."

Insurance companies and the government promised to help pay for the losses, but most people still lost many thousands of dollars. What they gained, however, was the knowledge that strangers could become good friends in times of need.

THE HURRICANE THAT COULDN'T HAPPEN

Most Canadians feel safe from the weather inside their homes, and so we should. Our houses are strong and sturdy to withstand snow loading from Canadian winters, and are well insulated to keep out the cold. But many well-built Canadian homes in the Toronto area were no match for a hurricane.

Hurricane Hazel began over Grenada, in the Caribbean Sea, in October 1954. It was the eighth hurricane that year and by far the largest. Its storm winds covered an area 1,500 kilometres wide, devastating Haiti and the American southeast coast. After ten days of destruction, it made an unpredictable turn inland, crossing the Adirondack Mountains in New York and hitting Ontario full force on October 15.

Almost everyone was caught off-guard. There had been warnings on the radio, but people paid little attention. After all, hurricanes were for the Atlantic coast, not Toronto.

Hurricane Hazel struck at midnight, dropping a record-breaking eighteen centimetres of rain in just twenty-four hours. This was about three times more rainfall than a bad rainy day in Toronto, and the result was deadly. Toronto had just gone through weeks of rainfall and the ground was like a soaked sponge. There was nowhere for the extra rainfall to go. Billions of litres of water followed streets and ditches downhill. Each overflowing ditch emptied into a racing creek, and each creek poured into a monster river. Each river turned into a raging torrent of brown water with strong currents even the best swimmers would never have managed to survive. Many of Toronto's rivers and creek valleys flooded to three metres deeper than normal.

Bridges in Toronto's many river and creek valleys were covered in water, some torn loose by the water's power. Houses in low areas began to flood as well. A man living on Raymore Drive in Weston heard strange sounds and went downstairs to find his living room floor completely flooded and water rising up the stairs.

Some houses were lifted from their foundations and torn apart. Others floated downstream. Quick-thinking people escaped their homes and waded through rising water onto higher land. Others hesitated and ended up balanced on rooftops or on their cars, not able to swim through the swift-flowing water. Police and firefighters lined river banks, attempting to throw ropes to these helpless people as water levels continued to rise. The water reached many before the ropes did. Days later their bodies would be found downstream. At one bridge that was being overrun with water, firefighters tried to talk a man out of driving his car, across. The man insisted. The car was lifted off the bridge bobbing along on the water with the man and his family screaming for help. They all died.

Eight firefighters answered a call to rescue people trapped in a car near the Humber River. When they arrived, the

A family tries to gather whatever possessions they have after Hazel destroyed their home.

people were gone. The fire truck then became caught in the water. The firefighters climbed onto the roof of the truck as the water rose. When the truck began to roll over, they jumped and tried to swim for shore, but only three made it.

Eighty-one people died during Hurricane Hazel, including thirty-five residents of Raymore Drive. Clean-up after the storm took months. Dozens of houses and about fifty bridges in the Toronto area had to be rebuilt.

Laws were passed preventing anyone from living in low-lying areas in Toronto. The many river and creek valleys became an attractive network of parks instead. If another hurricane is ever predicted for Toronto, those who remember Hurricane Hazel will be sure to take it seriously.

THE SAGUENAY FLOOD

The summer of 1996 was supposed to be good for the Saguenay region in the heartland of Quebec. Tourism always brought many visitors, especially for whale-watching on the Saguenay River, boating on Lac St-Jean, and the many local festivals and celebrations. The town of Laterrière was celebrating its 150th anniversary and many events were scheduled.

But as often happens, the weather interfered with everyone's plans. Heavy rainfall had hit the area for weeks, and the many dams in the area were already full. On Friday, July 19, heavy rains continued until a record-breaking twenty centimetres had fallen in forty-eight hours. This was as much rain in two days as the region would normally get in a month. The authorities controlling dams on the rivers let the water flow out to prevent a backup of water. But at the Kenogami Reservoir, problems began. Cranes that were supposed to lift dam gates failed, keeping the dam from releasing the proper amount of water. Water on Kenogami Lake built up to incredible heights, then overflowed, sending millions of cubic metres of water toward the city of Chicoutimi. The water came like a tidal wave, washing out dams downstream and sweeping away houses. Radio stations warned people to leave low-lying areas.

Some lost more than houses. In La Baie, the swollen waters of the Ha! Ha! River triggered a mudslide that demolished the Paquet-Garceau home. Though the parents and one child escaped with their lives, young Mathieu and Andrea, aged nine and seven, were killed, despite the frantic efforts of twenty rescuers to dig them out.

The Quebec Provincial Police found bodies inside cars after people attempted to drive across washed-out roads. In the end, seven people died and $700 million of damage was done.

The Saguenay River surrounds a lone house.

The Canadian military came out and worked with heroic energy through the crisis. Helicopters were heard continually as people were rescued from homes and areas of high ground. Canadian Forces Base Bagotville became a temporary home to thousands of evacuated residents.

The flood also brought sympathy from the rest of Canada. Banks and organizations across the nation accepted donations for the flood victims. The Red Cross set a goal of $2 million. In no time, they had surpassed that, raising $22 million.

Reginald Gervais, a city councillor in Jonquière, who had voted "yes" in a separatist vote just a few months before, said, "You cannot help but feel more Canadian and appreciate being Canadian."

ONTARIO'S KILLER TORNADOES OF 1985

On May 31, 1985, the power went out just after 4 p.m. at the Jellco Packaging plant in Barrie, Ontario. One of the managers studied the black and stormy sky and guessed the power would not be back any time soon. He sent home seventy workers who were arriving for the afternoon shift. His decision saved lives.

That day, storm clouds covered a large part of central Ontario. The weather forecast warned of severe thunderstorms and hail. Then, near Rush Cove on the Bruce Peninsula, a narrow spout of a tornado formed in the greenish black clouds and spun down to the earth, tracing an aimless and destructive path, like the finger of an angry giant. Others began to form over central Ontario until by the end of the afternoon, at least thirteen separate tornadoes had been reported. These violent storms caused Ontario's worst death toll by tornadoes.

In Orangeville, a funnel cloud wrecked a shopping plaza in less than a minute. All fifteen stores were flattened, but miraculously nobody was killed. On a nearby street, unaware of what was happening, Debbie Molto recalled, "I heard the front door bang and I went out to close it. The wind was so strong I was pulled out onto the porch and I couldn't get back into the house. I was crouching down, I think. The noise was terrific. I got soaked in the driving rain and I remember seeing lots of hail and lightning. I wasn't really sure what was happening. Then the clouds disappeared and the sun came out. I was still in a daze and I was covered in mud and bits of fibreglass insulation. I walked to the neighbour's house across the street and I commented on the damage to her house. She said, 'Look at your house.' I hadn't turned around to see how badly it was damaged. Most of the roof was gone. She gave me some clothes to wear since I was a real mess."

Just west of Highway 24, near Orangeville, Harold and Bruce Wilson's beef cattle farm took a direct hit from a tornado. Almost all the buildings were torn apart and only one of their eighteen farm vehicles was left untouched. The rest were reduced to junk. In minutes, thirty years of work was undone. Luckily, the Wilsons and most of their cattle escaped with their lives. Their damage cost about $1.5 million.

In Barrie, a city of 45,000 people, a large tornado headed for factories, houses and a highway. Jellco Industries, now empty of employees, was reduced to a pile of twisted metal beams and knife-edged pieces of sheet metal. Many of the people living in townhouses on nearby Adelaide Street were home when the tornado hit and most of those homes were completely destroyed in moments. The area looked like it had been hit by a bomb, but miraculously nobody was killed. Because the tornado was rain-wrapped, nobody in the town saw it coming. Drivers on Highway 400 slowed and stopped as full-sized trucks ahead of them were halted and pushed sideways by violent winds. Some drivers could only hang on as their own vehicles were shaken, lifted up or flipped over. One man was sucked from his parked car and killed when it rolled onto him. Altogether eight people died in Barrie.

In the beautiful town of Grand Valley, another tornado tore down stately Amaranth Street and, in minutes, uprooted centuries-old trees and ravaged picturesque houses. Two people died.

In communities like Hopeville, Corbetton, Honeywood and Lisle, people ran to cellars to escape the deadly tornadoes, which eyewitnesses said sounded like freight trains. Luckily, most of the destruction was to trees, crops and property.

Twelve people died and 285 were wounded by the various tornadoes which ravaged small towns and cities in Central Ontario that Friday afternoon. It could easily have been worse. Two of the tornadoes set records for size and duration. One that formed in Egremont Township travelled northeastward, leaving an eighty-five–kilometre path of wasted farmland, trees and buildings. Even longer was the path of a tornado that began in Arthur and meandered ninety kilometres before dissipating at Holland Marsh. The combined cost of all the tornadoes was about $100 million.

A boy looks at the remains of his home after a tornado tore through parts of Barrie, Ontario.

Barrie executed its emergency plan. City officials, police, hospital, firefighters and volunteers arrived at the worst-hit sites. A mobile command post was set up and members of a ham radio club provided communication since most telephone lines were down. Chaos turned to order as the people began the grim task of helping the wounded and finding those trapped in the rubble. First aid was provided by the Red Cross, and animal rescue volunteers rounded up pets that had fled collapsing houses.

The cleanup lasted for months. Three hundred Mennonite volunteers spent weeks helping tear down and remove the mess of what had once been homes. Other volunteers selflessly gave their time to help those who had been less fortunate.

One of the dead was a boy killed by flying debris while speeding down a road on his bicycle. He had been trying to escape the tornado. Parents used this tragedy to teach their children to seek shelter under stairs or in a basement, or even to lie in a ditch if a tornado strikes again. Being in the open is never wise. Although the likelihood of a tornado hitting your town is slim, it is always best to know what to do.

STORM OF THE CENTURY

Canadians in eastern Ontario, Quebec, New Brunswick and Nova Scotia will long remember the Ice Storm of

January 1998. It was the costliest storm in Canada's history, taking twenty-five lives and causing more than a billion dollars of damage.

In early January, unusual weather conditions brought first one, then a second storm of freezing rain to hover over the Ottawa and St. Lawrence valleys, one of the most densely populated areas of Canada. A glaze of ice covered every street and highway, making driving a nightmare. More than seventy millimetres of heavy ice, double the amount of a bad storm, coated everything.

Although the ice-coated trees sparkled with picture-postcard beauty, they were dangerous: large branches weighing hundreds of kilograms snapped like toothpicks, tearing down hydro lines, destroying cars and damaging rooftops. Whole lines of high voltage towers carrying power lines crumpled to the ground under the weight of the ice. Only one main major power line leading to Montreal remained upright, but barely. It was in danger of failing at any time.

More than two million people in the Montreal area were left without power. Millions more shivered in the dark in Ottawa, Kingston, Brockville, Quebec, Trois Rivières and Saint John, and in rural areas as far east as the Annapolis of Nova Scotia.

Downtown Montreal seemed almost deserted. Most businesses closed their doors as sheets of ice falling from buildings threatened people and damaged cars. All over the city, people stayed indoors.

Hydro towers, unable to support the weight of ice, lie crumpled in Quebec.

Students Joshua and Denise Trimm had a typical experience. "Our power went out for a full week. When it got too cold for us to stay at our house, we went over to our grandma's house because there was still power in that part of Montreal. Two days after we got there, our grandma's power went out, too. We slept with lots of clothes and blankets on. The next day the power came back on but the transformer outside our grandma's house exploded that afternoon and a neighbour's tree caught on fire . . . The home across the street had power and they invited us all in to keep warm. They let us watch cartoons, made soup for us and let us play with their grandchildren's toys.

"We have eight trees at our house, and some of the branches were hanging over the power lines. There was so much ice on the branches that they were bent all the way down to the ground.

"Dad went back to our grandma's house to make sure the pipes weren't frozen and he found that someone had broken in to grandma's house. They broke her back door down. Dad and Uncle Jimmy had to change her door. We had no school for two weeks, but we couldn't play outside because the falling ice and slippery streets made it too dangerous. We played indoors all day. We played cards and board games, read books, sewed and listened to the radio."

The ice storm had long-term consequences for Ruby and Jeff Hoogsteen of Alfred, Ontario. On a cold Wednesday evening they left a fire going in their fireplace and went with their five young children to a farm next door, helping a neighbour without power milk his cows.

"When we came home," Ruby says, "we smelled smoke, and Jeff found that fire was spreading from our fireplace to the wood beams in the basement. I took the children out of the house while Jeff tried to put the fire out. He couldn't, so we grabbed a few photo albums and waited outside. The local firemen could not put it out either and soon the whole house was burned to the ground.

"Still, the fire was a blessing . . . Neighbours and complete strangers helped us in the weeks and months that passed. Members of our church gave us everything we needed, a house to live in, kids' toys, clothes, toothbrushes and toothpaste, and even 200 rolls of toilet paper."

Some areas were without power for weeks, but help came from all directions. Fleets of public utilities trucks and hydro workers came from the Atlantic Provinces, Ontario, Manitoba and many American states to help with the repairs. These crews worked long hours for weeks in extreme cold and icy conditions, rebuilding towers, stringing almost 3,000 kilometres of new wire and setting more than 10,000 new poles in place. Thousands of electric generators were loaned or donated.

Years after the storm ended, the destruction to the larger trees is still easy to see. Few large trees escaped without damage.

Since the 1998 storm, many people have electrical generators just in case of an emergency. Those who lived through the "Storm of the Century" will not soon forget it.

DEATH ON THE MOVE

AIR INDIA FLIGHT 182

On June 22, 1985, at Vancouver International Airport, a man bought a one-way ticket from Vancouver to New Delhi, India. He gave a suitcase to the clerk, paid cash for the ticket and disappeared into the crowd, never boarding the plane. The suitcase was loaded onto a Canadian Pacific flight to Toronto. It would later be transferred to Air India Flight 182 jumbo jet flying to New Delhi. Inside the suitcase was a fake portable radio. Inside the radio was a bomb.

Just a few hours earlier the man placed a similar suitcase onto CP Flight 003 leaving for Tokyo, Japan, which would connect with an Air India flight to Bangkok. He did not get on board that flight either. The man was associated with an extremist Sikh nationalist group that wanted revenge on the government of India. He and others in his group were planning the mass murder of hundreds of innocent Air India passengers.

Air India had been warned of terrorist threats to their aircraft and had asked Canadian officials to x-ray the luggage going onto their flights to India. Despite the warning, airport security in Montreal failed to screen the luggage properly and the suitcase bomb was loaded aboard the Air India flight to New Delhi.

Flight 003 landed without incident in Tokyo, fourteen minutes ahead of schedule. The luggage was being transferred to the Air India jet when, at 3:19 p.m., a timer set off the bomb. Two Japanese baggage handlers were killed and four others were seriously hurt. Had it exploded while the jet was in the air, hundreds more people would have died.

Forty-five minutes later, Air India Flight 182 was over the Atlantic Ocean heading toward London. The flight carried two hundred and sixty-eight Canadians, twenty-seven Britons and twenty-four Indians as well as eleven people from other countries. The mood had been cheerful in Toronto and Montreal as families gathered at the airport to say goodbye to sons, daughters, husbands and wives leaving for vacation or business to India. Many of them were promising young teens, Canada's future leaders and artists. Most of the families had come to Canada from India years earlier and were returning to visit relatives.

The flight was going normally and the pilots had just contacted Shannon, Ireland's air traffic control centre. Then, two hundred kilometres from the coast of Ireland, the bomb suddenly exploded in the forward compartment, ripping open the aluminum skin of the jumbo jet. Travelling at hundreds of kilometres per hour, the 747 separated into several large pieces and spilled passengers into the air.

Neither pilot had time to send any sort of distress signal.

The remains of the aircraft and the bodies of the passengers plunged nine kilometres to the ocean below. Most of the airplane parts scattered and sank quickly, carrying bodies to the endless dark of the ocean floor.

Shannon air traffic control heard six seconds of a silent radio signal from the jet, indicating a microphone was open. Then Flight 182 disappeared from the radar screens. Other aircraft following the same flight plan were contacted but could not see it.

Search-and-rescue teams set out from Ireland, joined soon after by teams from Britain and Canada. Only bodies, lifejackets and some bits of luggage scattered over a wide area of the ocean, were found.

It was clear to investigators that the destruction was caused by a bomb. This explosion was soon connected to the one at Narita airport. In Japan, patient investigators worked for many days to find even the tiniest fragments of the bomb. They learned that it had been placed in the portable radio and found its serial number and model, tracing it to a small town in British Columbia. Meanwhile, investigators from Canada, Ireland and India sent mini-submarines down to the wreck of the Air India 747 in the Irish Sea. Seven hundred kilograms of aircraft pieces were recovered.

In Cork, Ireland, the local people opened their hearts to the grieving relatives as 131 bodies were brought in from the crash site. With caring words and acts of kindness, the Irish people, military and hospital officials helped the relatives deal with their first hours of grief.

Although intelligence agents in Canada had been following the activities of the terrorists and had much evidence against them, bringing them to justice took an extremely long time. A leader of the group, Talwinder Singh Parmar, was being investigated but was shot to death by police in Pakistan before he could be brought to Canada for trial. Others were arrested but, due to lost evidence, mistakes made by the police and prosecutors, and a lack of solid evidence, weren't convicted. The only person jailed was Inderjit Singh Reyat, who was found guilty of making the bombs. He pleaded guilty to manslaughter and was sentenced to fifteen years in prison. The trial of suspects in the Air India bombing was Canada's longest-ever trial, lasting almost twenty years and costing over $100 million. The Canadian Security Intelligence Service, the Royal Canadian Mounted Police and various government agencies were heavily criticized. Many blamed them for failing to prevent the bombing and then being unable to convict the terrorists. The lack of convictions against the terrorists has kept families of the dead from a feeling of closure.

The Air India bomb was the worst terrorist attack against Canadians, and with a total of 329 of all nationalities dead, one of the worst aircraft disasters of all time. Since the bombing of Air India Flight 182 and the September 11, 2001, terrorist attacks against the United States, airlines and airports all over the world have greatly improved security rules, making air travel much safer than in the past.

EXPLOSION ON FLIGHT 21

One of Canada's most important cold cases, or unsolved crimes, happened in 1965. Although it is Canada's second-worst aircraft bombing disaster, resulting in the deaths of fifty-two people, it is almost forgotten today.

Flight 21 was a regularly scheduled Canadian Pacific flight from Vancouver to Whitehorse, Yukon, flying through the summer skies of central B.C. Forty-six passengers and six crew members were on board the DC-6, a four engine aircraft. There was nothing about the flight that seemed unusual to the pilot, "Gentleman Jack" Steele of Vancouver.

More than 270 kilometres north of Vancouver, west of 100 Mile House, a sudden explosion in the left rear luggage compartment tore away the tail of the aircraft. The pilot was only able to radio a mayday three times before the aircraft's radio went silent.

Loggers working nearby heard an explosion and saw the DC-6 disintegrate. The tail separated from the body of the aircraft. The rest of the plane flew on briefly and then spiralled to the ground, spilling passengers and luggage over the heavily forested area. The wreckage of the plane burned on impact, and the tail landed 500 metres away. There were no survivors. About twenty of the people on board were found still strapped into their seats, many burned beyond recognition.

Crash investigators searched through the wreckage and soon found evidence that a bomb made with TNT or a similar explosive had gone off in the tail of the aircraft where much of the luggage was stored.

Aircraft were simple to board in the 1960s. In those more trustful times, luggage was not checked, nor were people examined for weapons or dangerous materials.

Royal Canadian Mounted Police officers investigated four passengers. Two of the passengers flying that day had access to large amounts of explosives. One of those had previously been charged with murder. Another passenger, an unemployed forty-year-old man, had taken out an insurance policy before the flight. It would pay his wife and children a large amount of money if the plane crashed. He was apparently flying north to take a job he'd been offered in a sawmill, but when police asked at various mills, nobody had heard of him. A fourth passenger, an accountant, was rumoured to have been threatened because he knew too much about somebody's financial troubles. That rumour was quickly disproven. The other suspects were investigated but, due to lack of evidence, nobody was ever identified as the bomber.

The crash site is still intact, about forty kilometres west of 100 Mile House, British Columbia. Plaques and mementos mark the places where family members have visited to leave some connection to their lost loved ones. Even after fifty years, there is hope that someone can solve the mystery.

THE CRASH OF SWISSAIR FLIGHT 111

On September 2, 1998, in the cockpit of a wide-bodied jet-liner, two senior Swissair pilots were struggling heroically to keep their aircraft flying level. Smoke was pouring down from the ceiling and they could barely see the instruments. The smoke and heat got worse. Aluminum began to melt above them, dripping down to the cockpit floor. Electric power began to cut out, causing instruments to fail. Captain Urs Zimmermann and co-pilot Stephan Loew couldn't even see out the window for visual references to help them fly, as dense clouds blocked the view. In spite of all these problems, the two pilots had managed to descend, dump extra fuel and make the several correct turns to approach Halifax airport, where neither of them had ever landed.

Halifax air traffic control had received an emergency request to land and had cleared the way for Swissair Flight 111. When the flight was last on the radar, it was over water, just minutes away from landing. But by 10:26 p.m., the radar contact disappeared. Flight 111 no longer answered the radio.

Shortly after 10:30 p.m., two fishermen, Cecil Zinck and Vincent Boutilier, were standing in the dark outside the Zinck home in New Harbour, Nova Scotia, when a passenger jet flew by low overhead. The aircraft was so low, Zinck wondered if his chimney was still on his roof. Moments later, they heard a tremendous crash on the sea. The men immediately went out in their fishing boats to search for survivors. Joining them were fishermen from Peggy's Cove and many other small harbours along the coast. They had all heard or felt the explosion and their only thought was to rescue the unlucky people involved. As ambulances from every community nearby raced to the shoreline, the fishermen did the first search, playing their flashlights on the water, calling out and endlessly trolling back and forth searching for survivors. Sadly, they found only remains of them: body parts, clothing, bits of wreckage, postcards and luggage.

Doctors Sandra Peacock and Stephen Sheehan were also dispatched to the government dock at Northwest Cove. Dr. Peacock had heard the explosion and felt her whole house shudder. They and a team of paramedics went out to try to help survivors of what they were sure was a major jet crash. They, too, found only bits of wreckage and body parts. For these would-be rescuers, the nightmare of the wreckage, human remains and the heartbreaking sight of children's toys and possessions floating on the water will stay with them all their lives. Experienced crash investigators said they had never seen such absolute destruction.

Part of an engine from Swissair Flight 111, found in the wreckage.

At the Queen Elizabeth II Hospital in Halifax, the emergency department had prepared for up to 200 injured passengers. Extra doctors, nurses and technicians had been called in. They waited for hours, sipping coffee and talking quietly before they were told they could all go home. Dr. Doug Sinclair, head of the emergency department, described it as a deeply sad moment. Of the 229 souls on the Swiss jet, not a single person had survived.

Swissair 111 was a regular flight from New York to Geneva, Switzerland. It was popular with American and Swiss tourists and with members of the United Nations. Included in the cargo of this flight were millions of dollars in cash, Swiss watches, diamonds and two original Picasso paintings.

When the wide-body jet aircraft crashed, it was torn into two million pieces, some no larger than a postage stamp. The passengers and crew were killed instantly, and the cargo was completely destroyed. Experts guessed the jet hit the sea at over 600 kilometres per hour, and at those speeds, hitting water is like hitting concrete.

Grieving relatives from the United States and Switzerland began arriving the next day, numb with shock. Peggy's Cove, the closest village to the crash site, is one of Canada's most photographed places. Its smooth-worn rocks, lighthouse and wood-frame houses have been popular tourist destinations over the years. Now hundreds of visitors to this tiny fishing port were American and Swiss families brought together by tragedy. The simple beauty of Peggy's Cove gave a small measure of peace to the families. Many people of Nova Scotia opened their homes to complete strangers, offered them meals, transportation or just lent an ear.

Dr. John Butt, the Chief Medical Examiner for Nova Scotia had had experience with disaster before as medical examiner for the Edmonton tornado. His was the hardest job: telling families that only DNA testing could establish true identity and nothing could be given yet for burial. Still, his sympathy for the grieving was an example to all.

Investigators discovered that faulty wiring from the new entertainment system caused the fire. Considering the failure of flight instruments and the intense fire and smoke, the plane were almost certain to crash. Changes in electrical wiring and materials were made immediately, but that is small comfort to the grieving families of Swissair 111.

VAN TRAGEDY IN ONTARIO

Juan Ariza and Javier Medina stared at the scenery around them. They were temporary farm workers from Peru and had just finished their first day on the job in Hampstead, Ontario. It was only their third day in Canada and they were enjoying their ride back to their residence after catching and vaccinating chickens at a poultry farm.

Their van was heading west on Line 47, toward the intersection with Perth Road 107. A large flatbed truck was driving south. As they approached the stop sign, Medina wondered whether their driver was going to stop or turn, but the van didn't slow down. Ariza locked eyes with the oncoming truck driver for a split second as the truck hurtled toward them.

The truck hit the side of the van at tremendous speed. There was an explosive crash and the van flew through the air, landing seventy-five metres off the road, its side completely torn off. Most of the thirteen men inside were thrown from the van. Beside the scattered bodies, the flat-bed truck lay overturned.

Ten of the van's passengers were killed, including David Blancas-Hernandez, the van's driver. All were temporary workers from Peru, except Juan Castillo, a Canadian. The driver of the other truck, thirty-nine-year-old Christopher Fulton, also was killed: it was his eleventh wedding anniversary. Blancas-Hernandez was also planning a trip home to celebrate his twenty-fifth wedding anniversary.

The three survivors, Ariza, Medina and Edgar Sulla-Puma, were badly injured. Sulla-Puma spent months in a coma.

Medina still has nightmares. He remembers one of his fatally wounded co-workers looking at him and pleading for help, but being too badly hurt to move.

Ariza remembers calling Medina's name over and over again. Medina assured him, "They're coming. They're coming," as they awaited the ambulance.

Police described the scene as horrific and were surprised anyone survived the crash. The fifteen-passenger

The van in which the Peruvian workers were travelling.

van was completely destroyed.

Immediate costs of hospitalization and funeral expenses were covered by insurance, but within hours, collections were organized for the families of the deceased as well as the survivors. Local unions and private donors gave to the "Migrant Workers Family Support Fund." Months later, cheques for about $15,000 each were given to Ariza and Medina and to the families of the men who died, most of whom came from the same village near Lima, Peru.

Investigators say the van's driver ran the stop sign. Some suggested the driver may have fallen asleep from fatigue; others guess the bright sunset may have blinded him as he drove west, preventing him from seeing the sign.

Investigators learned that Blancas-Hernandez wasn't licensed to operate a bus, which in Ontario is any vehicle designed to carry more than ten passengers. While having the correct class of licence wouldn't have prevented the accident, driving the right type of vehicle may have saved some lives.

Studies show that twelve- and fifteen-passenger vans are less safe in accidents than buses; doors on a van are much more likely to fly open and panels and roofs are ripped away easily. Van seats and seatbelts are also more likely to be torn loose than comparable seats and restraints in a bus. Protecting passengers should always be a priority.

THE "BOYS IN RED" TRAGEDY

On January 12, 2008, the weather was snowy and at times mixed with freezing rain, and the few drivers out past midnight in northern New Brunswick had slowed down because of slushy and icy conditions. Nearly home, the boys' basketball team from Bathurst High School, the Phantoms, was cheerful. As midnight passed, the team, also known as "The Boys in Red" because of their uniforms, sang "Happy Birthday" to Nick Quinn, who had turned sixteen. Everyone in the van had been up for hours, beginning with a regular school day, then a 225-kilometre drive to Moncton for an evening basketball game against the Purple Knights of Moncton High School and then the trip home again. The coach, Wayne Lord, was at the wheel of fifteen-passenger van. His wife, Beth, an elementary school teacher, was in the front seat. The couple's fifteen-year-old daughter was along for the ride as well, sitting behind her parents.

They were just ten minutes from home when Wayne felt the wheels go off the pavement and onto the right gravel shoulder. The edge drop from pavement to gravel was lower than it should have been, holding the tires on the gravel. Highway 8, though it had been sanded and ploughed a few hours earlier, was covered in three centimetres of slush. Wayne slowed and steered left, the tires eventually went back on to the road, but the van fishtailed and began to rotate counter-clockwise. Headlights showed an oncoming vehicle. Lord fought to correct the van's slide, but the van crossed the centre line of the road. The oncoming vehicle, a tractor-trailer, couldn't stop. Lord steered for the shoulder on the far left in a desperate attempt to avoid a collision.

It was over in an instant. The truck hit the van and, although both vehicles were driving slowly, the van was almost totally destroyed. Its right side was torn loose and most of the passengers were ejected. Killed by the impact were seven of the "Boys in Red" and Beth. The only survivors were Wayne, his daughter and two team members, Bradd Arseneau and Tim Daley. Daley was seriously injured.

The residents of Bathurst could hardly believe that seven students and a well-loved teacher had all been killed. Within hours, grieving friends erected a basketball stand with a wreath of flowers in the hoop as a makeshift memorial at the site of the accident. A tremendous outpouring of grief followed the tragedy, and the funeral service at the local hockey arena was attended by 6,000 people, including Canada's Governor General, Michaëlle Jean.

Transport Canada determined that the crash was caused by a number of factors: the weather and road conditions were poor; the drop-off from the road surface to the gravel shoulder was too great; the van was using all-weather radial tires instead of snow tires and it was in need of a brake adjustment.

Because fifteen-passenger vans have been found to give poor protection to passengers in a crash or rollover, some of the team members' parents appealed to the Province of New Brunswick to join many other provinces and American states in successfully banning the use of such vans for transporting students.

School boards all over Canada are returning to the use of school buses to transport children to team or club events. Although they cost more to buy and operate, school buses have safety windows and specially built doors that rarely open during collisions but can be exited easily in emergencies. School bus sides, floors and roofs have extra pillars and beams to increase strength. In fact, even school buses ready for the scrap heap are still so durable they often survive school bus races — which include rollovers — at racetracks across Canada.

THE CORMIER VILLAGE HAYRIDE

The McGraw and Leger families were having a yearly family reunion, celebrating Thanksgiving together on October 8, 1989. They met at the town hall of Cormier Village, forty kilometres from Moncton, New Brunswick. The family always enjoyed the traditional fall-colour ride on a hay wagon pulled by a tractor. In total, about fifty family members rode on the wagon and in two pickup trucks that followed. The autumn colours were beautiful as they slowly rode on the shoulder of Route 945.

But just a few hundred yards from the end of the ride, a lumber truck came around a corner. The truck lost control as it passed the wagon, and its load of six-metre-long logs shifted and spilled onto the hay wagon, crushing everyone. Thirteen people were killed and forty-five were injured.

Alcide Leger, a neighbour, was gardening nearby when the accident happened. He recalls the silence as he ran over to help. "Everything was quiet. Except for one little girl crying, everything was quiet."

Buried under piles of hay and fallen logs, a local priest was one of the victims of the crash. He recalled: "We were all talking, chatting, having a good time, and all of a sudden someone must have cried out 'It's going to hit us' or something like that," he said. "I raised my head and I remember the rolling logs — they were falling one at a time. I don't remember seeing the truck." After the crash the priest could recall only snatches of what happened — the wail of ambulances, people throwing bales of hay out of the way to get at the bodies and his search for his oils so he could give last rites to the dead and dying. "I was told that I did give last rites, but I can't remember to whom or how many."

Among the thirteen dead were five children and many families suffered multiple losses. Jean-Guy Leger, his wife, Simone and their six-year-old daughter Isabelle were among the dead. Dr. John Laba, a surgeon from Kentville, Nova Scotia, was killed, along with two of his four daughters: Jessica, age four, and Julia, age eight. His wife and two other daughters were injured but survived.

Emergency crews were quickly on the scene, helping those who were hurt or who had lost loved ones. The first responders were horrified. Nobody had ever seen this kind of loss before. After providing care and support to the grieving families, emergency workers and mental health professionals found they needed help themselves.

A year later, an inquest into the tragedy was held at the same community hall where the yearly reunion was held. Police investigators were certain the load of logs shifted before the truck lost control, and there were questions about how the load was secured. Regardless of who was to blame, nothing can bring back the missing family members of New Brunswick's worst road disaster.

THE BRIDGE THAT FELL TWICE

In 1900, a group of businessmen from Quebec City organized the construction of a bridge that would cross the St. Lawrence River. A famous American engineering firm seemed to have the best experience to handle the job. Their chief engineer, Theodore Cooper, oversaw the planning and design of the long and beautiful bridge. It was a cantilever bridge design, in which beams can extend long distances while supported only on one end. This bridge, once completed, would be the longest cantilever bridge in the world.

As construction started on the Quebec Bridge in 1907, Cooper noticed a serious mistake in the bridge design. It was not as strong as it should be. None of his fellow engineers had noticed it, but to point out the flaws now would mean long delays in rebuilding and extra cost. He was getting older and knew this would be his last major project. Cooper decided not to say anything, hoping that once the two ends of the bridge were joined together, it would be strong enough.

John Splicer was a high-steel construction worker and one of the best. He was from the Kahnawake Reserve near Montreal whose men were famous for their fearlessness and skill in working at great heights. While they usually felt confident, Splicer and many of his friends were not at ease working on the Quebec Bridge. As the horizontal deck extended across the river, one of the vertical steel beams was starting to bend. Engineers told foremen to bolt and rivet the beam straight, but the bend was getting worse every day.

Engineers became alarmed and in late August, one of them travelled to New York to inform Cooper. Cooper realized the weakness was showing after all and ordered work to be stopped, but the warning came too late: on August 27, while the engineer was returning to Quebec with the news, the bridge collapsed.

The middle of the bridge lies in the St. Lawrence.

John Splicer was not on the bridge that day. He had been too nervous and decided to stay home. But many of his friends and relatives were on the bridge when, almost at quitting time, chord A-9-L twisted around like a pretzel. In less than a second, support wires snapped, beams tore loose and the immense structure fell. Half of the bridge landed in the muddy waters of the St. Lawrence River, crushing or drowning those who were unable to jump away in time. Rescuers came immediately, but were unable to save men who were trapped in the wreckage. They could only watch helplessly as the water of the river began to rise with the tide, drowning the victims.

Seventy-five workers were killed, thirty-five from John Splicer's reserve. It was a devastating loss for the community.

The Quebec Bridge project was not abandoned. Nine years later, in 1916, a larger and stronger bridge was nearing completion. All that remained was for a large centre section to be hoisted in place from barges positioned in the St. Lawrence River. Cameras were set up to record the occasion. But as the centre section was being lifted into place, a corner section broke away. Twisting suddenly, the entire centre section fell onto the barges and into the water. Thirteen men perished.

People began to wonder if the bridge was cursed. Stories were told that the bridge was being built on sacred native burial ground. Others claimed that no bridge would ever span that part of the river. Finally, on September 20, 1917, another centre section was lifted from barges and carefully hoisted into place. The Quebec Bridge was finished, eighty-nine lives and seventeen years after it was started.

Two groups of Canadians will always remember "the bridge that fell twice": those of the Kahnawake Reserve and Canadian engineers. After losing so many men in their reserve in a single accident, the elders of the Kahnawake Reserve made the high-steel workers promise not to work all together on one job again. And because an engineer's mistaken calculations led to so many deaths, graduating engineers are given an iron ring as a reminder to always check their work. For many years the rings were made from one of the girders of the Quebec Bridge.

ST. HILAIRE BRIDGE DISASTER

William Burney was nervous. He had been a train engineer only eleven days when he was ordered to take a long train from Richmond, Lower Canada (now Quebec) to Montreal on June 29, 1864, on an unscheduled night run. The train was crammed full of people, immigrant workers speaking Czech, Polish and German, who had stepped off a ship from Europe the day before. Eleven freight cars had been hastily converted to coaches by installing wooden benches. They didn't even have windows. Nobody at the Grand Trunk Railway knew how many people were jammed into the cars. Some reports said 354 people were on the train, others, 475. The immigrants were herded in like cattle.

Burney had never driven the train on this route before and was unfamiliar with the signals. The train travelled westward for a few hours without incident. Then, for reasons that would be argued in court months later, the train ended up travelling too quickly as it approached a bridge crossing over the Richelieu River at Beloeil. The train bridge was open, allowing a tugboat to pull several barges through. Light signals ordered trains to come to a full stop, but the train continued forward. A combination of the tracks sloping downhill and the inexperience of the engineer brought the train of immigrant workers onto the open bridge.

The engine plunged over the opening and down, hitting a barge and tipping sideways into the river. The rest of the train cars followed the engine, one by one reaching the bridge and going over, each smashing whichever damaged car lay below it. The deafening crashes of rail cars drowned out the shouts and cries of pain as scores of passengers were injured or killed. Some leaped away from the cars but fell into the water and were drowned. Almost all those who survived had some type of injury.

Local residents and doctors from villages all around came to the rescue, pulling people out of the wreck. Great kindness was shown, despite the language barriers. The badly injured were taken to hospitals in Montreal, while those less seriously hurt were taken to local homes. Nobody knows exactly how many died because many bodies were never recovered from the river, but least ninety-nine of the train passengers died, along with most of the train crew.

The Grand Trunk Railway tried to avoid responsibility for cramming the cars full of people and sending a rookie to drive the train. They tried to pay the victims very little.

Some agents for the railroad even tried to get illiterate survivors to sign a legal form that excused the railway from any legal claim. The heartless attempts by the railway to avoid paying compensation was an outrage to the people of Lower Canada.

William Burney survived, but was fired by the railway and given the full blame for the disaster. For rest of his life he was shunned by adults and taunted by children for causing Canada's worst rail disaster.

CANADA'S CRUEL ARCTIC

Disasters in Canada's Arctic have the added feature of happening in incredibly remote places where the bitter cold in winter can kill a healthy adult in hours. Endless kilometres of rocky coastlines and ever-changing expanses of ice can cause adventurers, sailors or whole ships to disappear for days, or weeks or . . . forever.

FROZEN IN TIME: THE MYSTERIOUS DISAPPEARANCE OF THE FRANKLIN EXPEDITION

> *"Some of the bodies were in tents, others were under the boat which had been turned over to form a shelter, and some lay scattered . . . From the mutilated state of many of the bodies, and the contents of the [cooking pots] it*

is evident that our wretched countrymen had been driven to the dread alternative of canni-balism as a means of sustaining life . . ."
—John Rae, reporting what Inuit hunters found of the remains of Franklin's men.

Two hundred years ago, European explorers still knew very little about Canada's north. Though much of the world had been mapped out, nobody knew who lived in the Arctic or what it looked like. The rare ship that sailed into the frigid north found ice blocking the way or got trapped when winter came in September. Only whaling ships dared venture into the Arctic Ocean for a few short weeks in summer.

The mid-1800s were a rare time of peace for the British, with plenty of empty navy ships and restless navy officers eager to explore the world. The British government offered a cash reward to any navigator who could find a Northwest Passage — the long sought-after sailing route north of Canada's mainland from the Atlantic to the Pacific. This route would shorten the sailing distance to China and India. The reward was generous and led to dozens of failed Arctic voyages. The worst failure was the Franklin Expedition. Its two ships and 129 men were never found.

In the spring of 1845, Sir John Franklin, an experienced British Navy captain, set off, and determined to find the Northwest Passage, leading the best-equipped expedition of its time. It was his third attempt. Many years before, Franklin and a few dozen men tried to follow the Canadian Arctic coastline on foot. Poor planning and broken promises by Hudson's Bay suppliers led to starvation, murder and madness among Franklin's men. He and a handful of survivors were hours from death when they rescued by Copper Indians east of Great Bear Lake. Franklin became known as "the man who ate his boots," since he and his crew had eaten shoe leather to stay alive. Franklin led a second attempt to find the Northwest Passage by going down the Mackenzie River to the Arctic Ocean and mapping the ocean coastline. Though he and his men mapped hundreds of kilometres of the coast, extreme weather forced him to stop. This third time, Franklin, who had become a true hero of the people, would sail with over one hundred men in two sturdy ships and map out the missing parts of the Canadian coastline.

The two ships under Franklin's command, the *Erebus* and the *Terror*, were famous British gunships. Built to resist the recoil of many large cannons firing at once, they had wooden hulls over thirty centimetres thick and were reinforced with iron plates bolted across the bows as protection from ice. These sailing vessels were the first navy ships with steam engines, so they could power around ice packs in windless weather. The steam engines would also provide distilled water for drinking and steam heat for the lower decks, an unheard-of luxury.

Franklin's ships were well supplied. Each ship carried enough provisions for several years. Much of their food was stored in the latest of technology: tin cans. Can openers hadn't yet been invented so cooks would knock the lids off with a hatchet and mallet. Canned foods kept fresher than the traditional salt beef, salt pork, rum and maggoty biscuits. And fresh food was known to prevent scurvy, the deadly illness that plagued many sailors on long voyages.

On July 26, 1845, Franklin's ships met some whaling ships in Baffin Bay. They asked about weather conditions and sea ice.

That was the last official sighting of the Franklin expedition.

It was discovered later that Franklin's ships sailed west more than 1,500 kilometres, passing between Baffin and Devon Islands. They reached Beechy Island, where inscriptions on three lonely graves, and litter, including a pile of empty tin cans, tell of a winter spent there. A plateau of rock gave some protection from the groaning slabs of sea ice that could crush a ship. The long Arctic winter was passed indoors, with men working in lamplight to scrub the decks, repair gear and venturing out to chop holes in ice for water. Water was always needed because a fire on the ship was a sailor's greatest fear. Though it was seldom warm enough for the mariners to venture out to hunt for fresh meat, they were too far north to find game anyway.

On New Years' Day of 1846, a boyish twenty-year-old

coal stoker on the *Terror*, John Torrington, died. His shipmates hacked for hours through the iron-hard frozen ground to bury the young man's remains. Just three days later, John Hartnell of the *Erebus* died suddenly as well. Ninety days later another man from the *Erebus*, a mariner named William Braine, also died.

When the summer thaw melted the sea ice, Franklin's two ships sailed south but got only a few hundred kilometres before getting trapped in September sea ice. Now

The skulls of some of those who died on the Franklin expedition.

they were in a much worse location than the winter before, being forty kilometres from the shore of King William Island and exposed to the bitter wind. Both ships would also be at the mercy of the kilometres-wide expanses of sea ice that sometimes shifted and crushed ships. The two ships spent their second winter there.

It was normal for British navy ships on exploration missions to leave dozens of messages giving their location and progress for other ships to find. But only two messages about Franklin's expedition were ever found. The first note, left in a cairn of piled rocks on King William Island in May of 1847, described the first winter at Beechy Island and the second winter spent off King William Island. It said, "all was well."

But just a few months after that hopeful message, all was not well. Franklin died in June of 1847 and the leadership of the expedition passed to Captain Crozier of the *Terror*. Worse, the summer thaw of ice never came. Sunshine warmed the air, taunting the men with the possibility of sailing on, but the ice held fast. Winter returned in full force by September. Not only were the men trapped in the same location for another winter, but more of them began to die.

According to a second note left a year later, nine other officers and fifteen of the crew also perished. The cause of death was not given. The final part of the message, written in shaky handwriting, revealed that the men had abandoned the ships and were heading south for Back's Fish River (Back River). This meant a nearly impossible journey of almost 1,000 kilometres over the ice and through the most barren land imaginable.

Years later, at various places along the shore of King William Island, searchers found skeletons, heavy wooden rowboats and jumbled piles of useless items such as books, curtain rods and iron stoves. Sailors from the two ships apparently took much effort to drag almost everything of value across forty kilometres of ice. Why did they abandon their ships? Were the ships in danger of sinking? How would curtain rods and books help the men survive?

At least one group of about forty men journeyed to the southern end of King William Island. They were seen in July 1848 by Inuit hunters who gave the starving men a small seal — all the food they could spare. One hundred kilometres farther, having reached Canada's mainland, thirty-five or forty men camped at what is now named Starvation Cove on the Adelaide Peninsula.

Meanwhile, years had passed and the British public heard no news about their hero, Franklin. Five years after his crew had set sail, a large reward was offered for the rescue of Franklin or for finding his ships. Many expeditions went to search for them. Many famous Arctic explorers sailed from the east and the west. Some of these ships themselves became trapped in ice, with sailors starving or suffering from scurvy before their crews were rescued. Still, nobody could find Franklin. In England, Lady Jane Franklin used her considerable money and influence to hurry the search, but without success.

Dr. John Rae travelled overland to search for the Expedition in 1854, nine years after Franklin and his men set out. Rae had learned to survive the Arctic by living and travelling as the Inuit and Northern Cree did. He also spoke their languages. Rae found the isolated group of Inuit who had met Franklin's men on King William Island. They had spoons and silver plates engraved with the names of officers from Franklin's expedition, and Rae traded to get these items back. The Inuit told of meeting the starving white men some years before. The men said they were heading south to a Hudson's Bay outpost. Months later, the Inuit had found their skeletons on Starvation Cove. As the Inuit described it, some men had died as they walked along, and others died in a small camp. There was evidence some had cooked and eaten their dead comrades.

Rae returned to Britain and reported what the Inuit had told him. People despised Rae and refused to believe that any British sailor would resort to cannibalism. Rae returned the engraved spoons and plates he had bartered for, but the families suspected that the Inuit had murdered and robbed their men.

In 1984, researchers from the University of Alberta dug up the three frozen graves on Beechy Island from Franklin's first winter. Buried in extreme cold and still frozen, the bodies were perfectly preserved, looking like they'd been dead a few days instead of 138 years. Two of the men's lungs showed signs of tuberculosis, and all three bodies showed high levels of lead. The lead they were poisoned with came either from the poorly soldered tin cans or from the lead pipes that carried the drinking water on the ships. Little was known about lead poisoning in Franklin's day, and it could easily have been mistaken for scurvy. The cure for scurvy was fresh food, so the men suffering from lead poisoning were likely given more canned food, tainted with lead solder, as a cure.

The Franklin expedition is Canada's greatest exploration tragedy and the details remain mostly unsolved. The search is still going on. Parks Canada and the Canadian Coast Guard are doing underwater sonar scans to try to find the wrecks of the *Erebus* and the *Terror* during the brief summer seasons.

FIRST AIR FLIGHT IN RESOLUTE BAY

Some of Canada's most northern Arctic islands, remote places where Sir John Franklin and his men struggled through the long winters, are now home to small communities. These places can only be reached by ship during the brief northern summer; otherwise people come and go by aircraft. Such a town is Resolute Bay on Nunavut's Cornwallis Island.

Resolute Bay's airport is suitable for many types of

aircraft. The main runway has an electronic guidance system to allow planes to land in poor visibility. But even with modern equipment and experienced pilots, things can go terribly wrong.

On August 20, 2011, a Boeing 737 carrying freight and passengers was arriving from Yellowknife. First Air Flight 6560 approached the main runway using the electronic guidance system. Fog and rain reduced visibility and the pilots were unable to see the runway as they approached. Less than two kilometres from the airport, the 737 crashed into a small hill, killing all four crew members and eight of the eleven passengers.

The three who survived the crash were thrown free when the plane broke up. Twenty-three-year-old geologist Nicole Williamson told CBC's Peter Mansbridge what happened. Although it was quite foggy, the jet was flying normally as they prepared to land. She heard the landing gear lock into place. Suddenly the 737 broke into pieces, separating just ahead of Williamson's seat. ". . . it came apart exactly where I was sitting . . . When a plane comes apart you see the wires and metal . . . you feel everything just falling apart around you." Williamson threw her arms in front of her face for protection and then found herself rolling along the ground, still buckled to her airplane seat. "I was rolling and tumbling through all this stuff and just couldn't understand why I was still conscious . . ."

When she stopped rolling, Williamson was dazed and in

pain. A fire was burning the remains of the tail. Except for the sounds of fire, all was silent. Then she heard the crying of seven-year-old Gabriella Pelky, a girl she had befriended at Yellowknife airport. Pelky had cuts on her face and her leg was obviously broken. Williamson helped her over to a small hill where they awaited rescue. The only other survivor was Williamson's co-worker, forty-eight-year-old Robin Wyllie. Wyllie was injured and in pain, but conscious.

A crew of firemen from Resolute Bay arrived within a few minutes and began to give first aid. Soon after, a helicopter landed carrying military search and rescue personnel. More arrived on all-terrain vehicles.

Normally search-and-rescue teams take hours to get to a plane crash, especially so far north. But the military had just come to Resolute Bay to participate in a yearly exercise called "Operation Nanook." More than 1,100 specialists in various fields were involved in a mock aircraft disaster. Once it was clear a civilian 737 jet had actually crashed just a few kilometres from the airport, they stopped the exercise. Communications informed them this was a "no duff" situation, meaning this it was real and not an exercise.

The three survivors were given immediate attention at a temporary emergency room at the Resolute Bay airport, which medical personnel had prepared for multiple casualties. Soon they were transported to the hospital in Iqaluit. Williamson was not yet aware what had happened to the passengers. It was a shock to find there were no other survivors beside Pelky and Wyllie. Williamson had a shattered foot and a broken pelvis, but was grateful to be alive.

The twelve who died were likely killed instantly. Pelky lost her six-year-old sister Cheyenne in the crash. Two of the passengers killed had a fear of flying, which came from having survived a previous airplane crash in Nunavut. The older of the two men, Michael Rideout, had even been involved in another plane crash in Labrador thirty years previously. Family members would recall how difficult it was for either man to board an aircraft. A third passenger had avoided flying all his life, also from fear.

Another passenger who lost his life was an Arctic researcher and director of Canada's Polar Continental Shelf Program, Marty Bergmann of Winnipeg. Bergmann was supposed to give Prime Minister Stephen Harper a tour of a new Arctic research facility the following week.

An official investigation into the crash is still ongoing. Hopefully the answers will give comfort to the people of Resolute Bay and families of the passengers and crew of First Air Flight 6560.

MEDICAL DISASTERS

Canada's worst killers have not been wars or violent storms, airplane crashes or even the Halifax Explosion. Many more Canadians have died tragically because of microscopic killers that live all around us.

Viruses are too tiny to be seen with a regular microscope, yet are as old as life itself. Most viruses are harmless, not quite alive and not dead either. They exist on and in every sort of plant or animal. Some viruses can be harmful, causing illnesses like the common cold, chicken pox or cold sores. Much worse are deadly viruses that cause polio, rabies, AIDS, the flu or SARS. These viruses have killed millions of people.

Bacteria also co-exist with us. The human body has ten times as many bacteria living on and in us as the number of cells in our body. Bacteria can usually be seen through a microscope and, while some are good for us, such as those that help us digest food, others can be harmful. Bacteria cause things like food poisoning, pneumonia and tuberculosis.

The following stories tell of Canadians who were harmed or killed by these tiny enemies. The heroes are the careful medical professionals, nurses and doctors, researchers and technicians who spent hours treating the sick, identifying the cause of their illnesses, and tracking down the proper remedies or cures.

POLIO: THE CHILDHOOD CRIPPLER

Eleven-year-old Ken Cleverdon waited by the rink, rapping his stick against the boards, waiting to play. He wore brand new equipment: a Maple Leafs jersey, matching blue hockey pants, socks and new skates. The older boys looked at him with pity. One of them whispered, "He shouldn't play. It's not fair to him." Another boy snickered, "His right leg is like a matchstick. He'll just break it." Cleverdon had a shriveled leg from when he had polio at age three. Cleverdon knew he was weaker than the others, but he told himself, "I'm going to do it. I'm going to prove to them I can do it." Cleverdon climbed over the boards and onto the ice, wobbled and almost fell. The other kids were faster. He didn't care; he began skating after the puck.

In the first half of the 1900s, one of the most feared diseases in Canada was Infantile Paralysis, or Poliomyelitis: polio, for short. It usually struck children and was most common in the warm summer months.

Most people who caught polio never had serious effects. They might feel a fever or achy limbs or a headache for a few hours. But for the five percent who were seriously affected, polio could cripple or kill.

In victims like Ken Cleverdon, who spent months in the hospital, the virus attacked the spinal cord and weakened the nerves leading to muscles. Within hours, the person was barely able to move. Some stayed paralyzed for months and their legs or arms had to be kept in splints to prevent deformities. After some rest, about half regained use of their limbs, and many recovered fully. But some were left crippled, often with one leg or one arm thinner and much weaker than the other. A few never regained use of their muscles and were confined to a wheelchair for life.

The deadliest polio, bulbar polio, attacked the muscles used to breathe and killed many people. Then the "iron lung" was invented: patients would lie in coffin-like machines with only their heads sticking out. Inside, the air pressure changed rapidly, allowing the victim to breathe. Toronto's Hospital for Sick Children was overwhelmed in the 1937 polio epidemic when dozens of children came in with respiratory failure. The hospital had only one iron lung, imported from Boston, and couldn't get new ones for weeks. Canadian engineers began to build their own, and soon Sick Kids had thirty-five iron lungs in use day and night.

In some years, Canada had higher rates of polio than any other country in the world. In 1953, there were 8,878 cases of polio and 490 deaths. Polio rates in the Prairies and Ontario were the highest. Children would come down with aches and stiff muscles or weakness. If a test of spinal fluid showed that polio was present, the child would be rushed to the nearest hospital that had a polio ward. Treatment for polio victims was paid for by the local government.

Nobody knew how polio was passed on, but everyone

had a theory. Most parents kept their children from crowds. Playgrounds, beaches, sports fields and parks across Canada were almost deserted in summer. Other people suspected mosquito bites or flies, dog ticks, cold drafts, hot breezes, too much exercise, too little exercise, sitting up straight or sitting slumped. But nothing seemed to prevent polio. Only the onset of cold weather produced a drop in infections.

All over the world, medical scientists tried to create a polio vaccine. Vaccines are a tiny mixture of a weak or dead virus that is injected into a healthy person's body. The body fights off the weak virus and creates antibodies to recognize and fight the infection in the future. Vaccines save lives all over the world, but making a safe vaccine is very dangerous work. If the vaccine is too strong, it can sicken or kill healthy people with the very disease it is supposed to protect against. If the vaccine is too weak, it won't give protection to the person needing it.

After decades of failure, American researcher Jonas Salk finally succeeded in making a polio vaccine in 1954. The news made headlines all over the world and made Salk famous. Connaught Laboratories of Toronto was the first to produce this vaccine in large quantities.

But just as long-awaited vaccinations began in 1955, a tragedy unfolded. One of the companies in the United States made the vaccines incorrectly and gave polio to hundreds of healthy children. Dozens died. The American government immediately halted the vaccination program.

Canada's Health Minister, Paul Martin Sr., was under extreme pressure to stop the Canadian vaccinations, too. Martin, like his son, was also a polio victim. But he trusted the Connaught vaccine and took the courageous step to allow Canadian children to continue to get vaccinations. History proved him right. The Canadian vaccine was safe, and Canadian children became immune to the polio virus a year ahead of those in other countries.

By 1957, Alfred Sabin had perfected an oral vaccine which made it even easier to fight polio.

Polio is still with us, and people who haven't been vaccinated can still get the disease. All Canadian children are supposed to get five vaccinations in their early years. These vaccinations protect them from polio, diphtheria, tetanus and whooping cough. These diseases still cause illness and death in countries that do not have regular vaccination programs.

In recent years, an illness called Post-Polio Syndrome has struck twenty-five to fifty percent of people who were child sufferers of polio. It happens to adults between thirty-five and sixty years of age, causing weakening of the muscles damaged by polio many years before. Doctors are not sure why this occurs.

Ken Cleverdon is an old man now, but he remembers his treatment for polio like it was yesterday. "The six weeks I spent at Sick Kids felt like a lifetime. I was kept in isolation and away from my parents. The kind nurses and doctors became my family during that time. When it was time to go home, I cried because I didn't want to leave them. There's always been a spot in my heart for Sick Kids."

2008 LISTERIOSIS OUTBREAK IN ONTARIO

In July of 2008, an eighty-nine-year-old resident of a nursing home in Ontario came down with a sudden illness. She had a fever, muscle aches and was vomiting; all serious symptoms for an elderly person. When the sickness didn't clear up, she was taken to the hospital, but she died two days later. Doctors noted that she had listeriosis, an illness in the bloodstream caused by the common listeria bacteria. Blood tests showed that another sick resident of the nursing home had the same bacteria.

The listeria bacteria is very common, infecting many people every year. The bacteria are found on plants and in soil and will often grow on food left in a refrigerator too long. Cooking foods properly kills the bacteria. Food infected with listeria may not look, smell or even taste bad. In fact, every day, some healthy adults eat food containing listeria and don't get sick at all. A few get a queasy stomach or diarrhea.

But listeria bacteria *can* kill. One in five patients dies of the disease. It is particularly dangerous to people who are already ill, the elderly or newborn babies. In pregnant women, listeriosis may cause premature delivery, infection or death of the unborn baby.

In the summer of 2008, Public Health officials in Toronto noticed an increase in reported listeriosis illnesses. While normally four or five cases of listeriosis may be reported in a month, seven or eight were reported that June; the elderly woman was the first death. Officials thought that the infections might come from a single source. Health Canada investigated the residence's kitchen, which was clean, and then the meat products eaten by the residents. Studies of the bacteria showed it came from cold meat products that were already contaminated when they were bought.

By mid-August 2008, Maple Leaf Foods of Toronto was warned that some sliced meat products were being investigated as the source of listeria bacteria. The head of Maple Leaf Foods, Michael McCain, made sure warnings were sent to their customers not to serve or use the sliced roast beef and corned beef that were suspected.

Other health units in Ontario began reporting an unusual increase in listeriosis cases. Maple Leaf Foods recalled twenty-three different meat products, removing them from store shelves. The investigation found listeria bacteria on slicing machines on Line 8 and Line 9 of the Bartor Road food plant in Toronto. The plant was shut down for thorough cleaning.

More cases of listeriosis were reported and more people died. Even though stores recalled the suspected meat, some infected meats which had been sold earlier were already in people's refrigerators or had been made into ready-to-eat deli sandwiches for sale in food stores. And some people can have listeria virus for weeks before it finally made them sick, which makes it difficult to find out what foods caused their illness. By the end of August, fifteen deaths were being investigated. By then there were twelve suspicious deaths in Ontario, and one each in Quebec, British Columbia and Saskatchewan.

Maple Leaf Foods increased their recall to over 200 types of meat products. These were sold under many different brand names all across the country.

McCain issued a public apology, accepting responsibility for the tragedy and offering deepest sympathy. He assured the public that the company would do all it could to make production at Maple Leaf Foods safe again. Business leaders seldom accept blame as openly as McCain did, but Canadians appreciated his honesty.

Meanwhile, the media wondered why government inspectors hadn't noticed the problems with the food preparation process. The president of the Agriculture Union blamed federal government cost-cutting for food inspectors. A study by CBC and the *Toronto Star* found that inspectors spent less than two hours daily at the Maple Leaf Foods Bartor Road plant. Some visits lasted under fifteen minutes.

Newspaper articles recalled how deaths from untreated well water in Walkerton, Ontario, happened after government cutbacks resulted in city well water not being tested by provincial inspectors. The federal government promised an investigation into the deaths from the listeriosis outbreak.

By the end of 2008, twenty-two people across Canada had died as a result of listeriosis from the Maple Leaf Foods plant. Maple Leaf Foods agreed to pay out $27 million to their families.

The outbreak of listeriosis was a painful lesson to Canadians and to the food industry.

SARS IN TORONTO

The animal cages in the market were filthy. Dozens of animals, including turtles, snakes, goats, chickens, frogs, giant salamanders and civet cats, were kept in dirty cages stacked on top of each other in an open market in Guangdong Province, China. Some of these animals were sick, their feces, blood or saliva infected with strange viruses. Viruses usually live in only one type of animal and cannot spread to another species. On this day, however, one of the viruses mutated, or changed, enough to pass on to humans. These caged animals were to be sold to restaurants. Some people believe eating the meat of exotic animals gives certain healing powers, but instead, one of these animals brought death.

Sometime in December 2002, a market worker who fed the animals or moved the cages and who researchers would later only know as "patient zero" must have inhaled microscopic droplets of this new virus from the sneeze or cough of an affected animal. The mutated virus began to reproduce itself in his body. Within a few days he began to feel sick. By the time he went to a doctor, he had been coughing for several days. The doctor thought he had pneumonia and treated him for it, but the treatment didn't help.

Other workers from the Guangdong market began to come to the hospital with high fever, shortness of breath and muscle aches. They were also treated for pneumonia and given antibiotics, and they too got worse. Family members of the sick began to show the same illness, as did doctors and nurses who treated them.

By January 2003, some of these people began to die. Doctors were stumped. People seemed to be sick with a deadly new form of pneumonia. But while pneumonia does not spread from person to person, this disease was very contagious. They warned the local health department that they had a new illness, probably a virus, that they knew almost nothing about. There seemed no way to treat it, and it was spreading fast. At first the Chinese Government tried to keep it secret. They didn't want to discourage travellers or tourists from coming to the popular Guangdong vacation area.

Unfortunately, the illness had a long incubation time, meaning people would carry the virus for several days before feeling ill. Tourists who got infected didn't feel sick or start sneezing until they had returned home to other parts of China, carrying the new virus with them.

In February 2003, Dr. Liu Jianlun from the Guangdong region went to a wedding in Hong Kong. While staying at the popular Metropole Hotel, he developed a fever and an uncontrollable cough. Suspecting he had gotten this new, untreatable illness from one of his patients, he warned the doctors and nurses in the hospital to wear masks and gloves when examining him. This saved their lives, but more than twenty people who had shared an elevator with him in the hotel or attended the wedding were infected with the new virus.

While doctors in Hong Kong tried to treat Dr. Jianlun, news spread that the Chinese were dealing with a new and mysterious killer virus. The doctors in Hong Kong realized they were seeing the same illness as in mainland China, but it was too late to control the outbreak. Many of the hotel guests had already left for homes in Singapore, Vietnam and Toronto, bringing along a deadly souvenir.

Researchers identified the virus as a type of coronavirus, a circular virus with points around the edge, looking like a crown. It resembled a cold virus. The disease was given a new name: Sudden Acute Respiratory Syndrome, or SARS. Dr. Carlo Urbani of Hanoi, Vietnam, the man who first identified and named SARS, soon died of it.

At the same time, a seventy-eight-year-old Toronto woman who had visited relatives in Hong Kong became ill, dying five days later. Her son became sick as well and died in a Scarborough hospital eight days later. Doctors in Toronto, assuming the woman had pneumonia, had not isolated either the mother or the son. Family members who visited them, as well as other patients who'd sat in the emergency rooms with them in the same hospital, began to get sick. Even more worrisome was that some health-care workers who had treated them came down with the same illness, even though they had worn masks and gloves. Within weeks Toronto was seriously affected by SARS.

Ontario health authorities asked the World Health Organization for help. Toronto now had the largest number of confirmed cases in North America. The news media reported it and suddenly people got very nervous. Anyone who may have travelled to Hong Kong or China was suspected of having the virus and were told to call their doctors and stay in their homes for at least ten days. Chinese restaurants were almost deserted. Medical workers who might have been exposed were required to avoid public areas and crowds and wear masks when in public.

The World Health Organization declared Toronto a high-risk destination and advised people not to travel there. Toronto's reputation as a safe tourist destination disappeared overnight. Tourism halted almost completely and people leaving through Pearson International Airport were screened for traces of illness.

Toronto health-care workers had a very difficult time. Not

only were they in danger of getting the disease, but they also had to work extra-long shifts to help fight it. Because ordinary masks and gloves didn't seem to offer enough protection against SARS, doctors and nurses had to wear additional face shields and gowns to protect themselves and their patients. Overworked nurses and doctors were also not allowed to sit together in lounges or eat together during breaks, making their days seem even longer and more depressing.

Some hospitals closed their doors to new patients, and all visitors had to be screened by medical staff before they entered the building. In some Toronto hospitals no visitors were allowed at all unless the patient was likely to die within a day. Even then, only one relative was allowed to stay with the dying person. Heartbroken families had to decide who would spend the final hours with a beloved relative.

All over Canada, hospitals were put on alert and restrictions were made. Any patient with a cough or flu-like symptoms was put in isolation or told to stay home.

Slowly the number of SARS cases diminished until, in May 2003, it was believed all cases of SARS in the Toronto area were known and being treated. The World Health Organization lifted the travel ban to Toronto and hospitals relaxed some of their rules. That was a tragic mistake.

SARS broke out again, because two patients with undetected symptoms were allowed to leave the hospital. These people's coughing spread new cases of SARS to seventy-eight others. Once again a travel ban to Toronto was issued and restrictions in the city's hospitals became stricter than ever. It was another seven months before SARS was under control in the Toronto area.

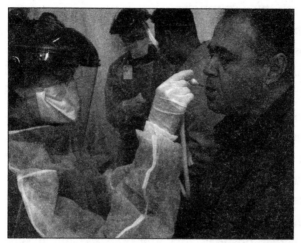

Staff are examined before entering Toronto Western Hospital.

Forty percent of those who caught SARS were nurses, doctors, technicians hospital and cleaning staff. Doctors were especially at risk when putting a breathing tube down a SARS patient's throat.

In July 2003, the Rolling Stones headlined a benefit concert in Toronto that raised money for victims of SARS. The concert helped restore Toronto's reputation as a safe place to visit. Half a million people attended the SARS benefit concert, also known as "Toronto Rocks," making it the largest rock concert in Canada's history. It was a great success.

In the end, forty Canadians died of SARS, including two nurses. The worldwide death toll was much worse. By the end of 2003, there were 774 dead out of 8,098 reported cases in twenty-nine countries.

Every year the flu kills many more people than this. So why is SARS such a disaster?

Unlike yearly flu epidemics, which usually kill people who are already sick or very old, the SARS virus killed people who were normally healthy. But more importantly, the epidemic showed how easily a common virus could mutate into something new and deadly to humans. SARS reminded medical people how very difficult it can be to identify and defend against new viruses, especially with so much worldwide travel.

Canadian hospitals are better prepared, but an illness like SARS can easily come again.

THE SPANISH FLU

The general store at Paradise Hill, Saskatchewan, sat empty except for the dead bodies of the storekeeper and his wife. Inside a nearby tent there were three more victims. The eerie silence was only broken by the sounds of a young boy digging graves for his dead mother, father, brother and sister.
— Battleford Press, *November 28, 1918*

World War I caused the violent deaths of millions of soldiers, but as the war ended, a worse killer followed. The Spanish Flu epidemic of 1918 killed about sixty million people around the world. For many years it was almost forgotten, although one in six Canadians caught the Spanish Flu and more than 50,000 Canadians died of it.

Recently scientists have begun to study the Spanish Flu again. Now they believe it was a type of influenza virus that crossed from pigs to birds and then to humans. Soldiers in got the virus first. It spread quickly because they lived close together in filthy trenches and travelled in crowded trains and ships. By the time sick soldiers were hospitalized, they had already spread the virus to others. Healthy soldiers returning from the war were exposed to it while crammed together on troop ships. From major ports like Halifax and Quebec City, the virus followed the soldiers along rail lines and roadways to every town in Canada.

The flu had little to do with Spain, except that Spanish newspapers were the first to report the sickness truthfully. The countries fighting in World War I hid details of their own epidemics. A German general later admitted that a major battle was lost because so many of his soldiers were sick.

The Spanish Flu spread rapidly, overpowering the body's ability to fight off infection. It made everyone sick, but unlike most viruses, the Spanish Flu was deadliest to young and otherwise healthy people. The symptoms were fever, chills, headaches, sore throat, muscle pain and cough. Sufferers were sometimes too weak to move for three days or more. In serious cases, people coughed blood, their skin turned blue and they got pneumonia. Heroes of "The Great War" who had avoided death during battle were sometimes killed just a few days after getting infected.

Ethel Dickenson of St. John's, Newfoundland, served with distinction during the war as a nurse, and volunteered to help Spanish Flu victims on return. She caught the flu and died within weeks. Eighteen-year-old Alan McLeod of Manitoba earned the Victoria Cross for bravery as a pilot during the war. All of Canada heard how he shot down three aircraft in a dogfight, chased away four others and was seriously wounded. His plane caught fire, but he landed it while half standing on a wing to avoid the fire, and then dragged a wounded fellow officer away from the flaming wreckage. Days after returning to Canada as a war hero, he caught the Spanish Flu and died.

Some people died within just hours. Two girls sharing a room in the YWCA went out together in the evening. The next morning, Clare Hunter thought her roommate had slept in. But when she checked, the other girl was dead and cold.

The tragedy left many orphans. At Mountaineer Cove, Newfoundland, a tiny community of four houses, all the adults were found dead in their homes, lying where they had fallen. The survivors, five small children, were gathered in the kitchen of one house, managing by themselves, with dead adults lying nearby.

Across the whole country, hospitals and clinics were overwhelmed. As each town and city was infected, hundreds of people would be bedridden for at least three days, unable to help themselves. Businesses shut down and schools closed. There was a shortage of doctors and nurses since many were still serving overseas. The few medical professionals left behind worked day and night with little rest. Retired doctors and nurses were called back to help.

In 1918, doctors knew that germs spread disease from person to person. But they could detect bacteria with the microscopes in use at that time, they could not detect viruses, which are one hundred times smaller. When the Spanish Flu hit, they could only guess what caused it. They had no remedies, but could only try to keep it from spreading. In most communities, the Public Health Officers recommended people avoid crowded areas and wear masks in public. In some places they banned public meetings and closed schools, dance halls and theatres. Only when the electron microscope was invented in 1933 could researchers see that flu viruses are so tiny they can pass through gauze masks. Thirty million could fit on the head of a pin. Flu viruses also mutate, or change, frequently, making them harder to treat.

Even today the only way to stop the spread of flu remains to isolate people who have it, and make sure people get vaccinations.

In recent years, scientists have dug up frozen graves in the Arctic to find preserved Spanish Flu viruses in corpses so they can study them. As distasteful as this sounds, they know that an epidemic like the Spanish Flu could kill millions if it happened again.

THE WALKERTON WATER TRAGEDY

On Tuesday May 16, 2000, a few students at Mother Teresa School in Walkerton were ill. Some had painful stomach cramps and could not stop throwing up. A few had diarrhea. By Thursday, May 18, many more students were sick. Some had bloody diarrhea, which is always serious, and two of these children were sent to Dr. Kristen Hallett, a specialist in Owen Sound. Dr. Hallett suspected *E. coli* poisoning, which is also called "hamburger disease" because it can be found in undercooked meat. She ordered tests and alerted Walkerton health-care officials.

At the same time, more people with the same symptoms began to arrive at Walkerton Hospital. Because they were dehydrated, doctors sent them home with instructions to keep drinking lots of water. Some people with kidney damage were sent to larger hospitals nearby. Test results proved they were all suffering from a serious form of *E. coli* poisoning, called *E. coli* O157:H7, and another poisonous bacteria, *Camplylobacter jejuni.*

Various types of *E. coli* bacteria are commonly found in the intestines of animals and humans. These bacteria help us digest food. But *E. coli* O157:H7 can be deadly. It is a type of bacteria that has mutated and cannot be killed easily. It can cause severe intestinal problems and may lead to kidney failure and death.

Public health inspector David Patterson looked for the source of the outbreak. He learned that the sick people had not gone to the same restaurant or eaten the same food. All they had in common was that they lived in Walkerton or had recently visited. Because *E. coli* can also be found in untreated water, David Patterson called Stan Koebel, the manager of the Public Utilities Commission. He asked if the town's water system was okay, and if anything unusual had happened lately. Although he hesitated, Stan told David that everything was fine. He probably even believed it and kept drinking the water. But he was not telling all he knew.

A week before Patterson's call, Koebel had received a report from a laboratory showing that the water had high amounts of *E. coli* bacteria. Stan had managed Walkerton's water for years, and had seen bad reports before. Nothing had ever come of them. He guessed that if the water was bad enough to harm people, the lab would notify the Ministry of the Environment and the Health Department. That was how things had been done in the past. Unfortunately, new government rules did not require the laboratory to notify these departments.

Also, due to carelessness and poor training, Koebel and his co-worker and brother, Frank, hadn't been properly treating Walkerton's water. They put less chlorine into the water system than was required, and in order to save time they didn't take water samples from the proper locations. For years nothing bad happened, but a flood that spring caused high levels of bacteria from cattle manure to enter the water system. Normal chlorine treatment would have killed the bacteria, but this wasn't being done. Walkerton's water supply was poisoned. Soon the bacteria in the town's drinking water began to kill.

On May 22, Lenore Al, a cancer patient, died after being admitted to hospital with suspected *E. coli* poisoning. Two-and-a-half-year-old Mary Rose Raymond of Hanover, who had visited Walkerton on Mother's Day, died on May 23. Betty Trushinski, a healthy fifty-six-year-old who usually drank lots of water, passed away soon after. Kody Hammell, almost two years old, had to be flown to a London hospital. His kidneys were failing and his little body was badly swollen. Hundreds more in Walkerton were too ill to get out of bed. Others could not leave the washroom because they never stopped being sick. Parents, desperate to help their screaming children, were told to keep giving them lots of water and other fluids and to wait for them to get better.

Walkerton is an old and friendly town. Rumours travel

fast. More and more people began to suspect the water. Many stopped drinking it. Stan Koebel grew worried. Perhaps those failed bacteria tests were worse than he had thought. He spent the Friday and Saturday of a long week-end increasing the amount of chlorine in the wells and opening fire hydrants to flush out the main water pipes. Bob McKay, who worked for Stan, saw his boss flushing out the water mains. Suspecting the worst, he told his family to stop drinking the water. Then he phoned a government hotline to warn them about Walkerton's water supply.

Soon afterward, Public Health Director Dr. Murray McQuigge ordered television and radio stations to warn people to boil water used for drinking, cooking or bathing. Vast amounts of bottled water were trucked to the town. Citizens began what would become a months-long ritual of going to the local arena to pick up their drinking water.

Government of Ontario water experts took over the Walkerton water system and flushed out every water line on every street and in ever house. High amounts of chlorine were run through to kill any bacteria remaining. It still took seven months before the water in Walkerton was safe to drink.

Eventually, a public inquiry, led by Judge Dennis O'Connor, investigated the tragedy. Over a hundred wit-nesses were interviewed, including Ontario Premier Mike Harris. Judge O'Connor's report made it clear the trag-edy could have been prevented. His report found many

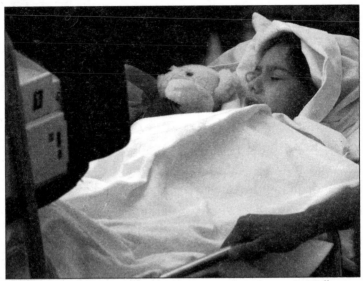
A little girl lies in hospital after drinking contaminated water in Walkerton.

groups of people responsible. Town officials had allowed a
well to be drilled in the wrong location years before. Stan
and Frank Koebel were guilty of poor work and keeping
false records. The Ontario Government was to blame for
cutting water inspectors and closing government laboratories. The Ministry of the Environment was at fault for not
enforcing rules for water treatment. Walkerton residents
also criticized the local health unit and the town council for
not announcing the boil-water advisory earlier and for not
making sure everyone knew about it.

For their mishandling of the water management system, Stan Koebel was sentenced to one year in jail and his

brother Frank to nine months of house arrest. Although their names were the most mentioned in news reports of the time, they were only part of the problem.

There have been many changes to the way water is tested and how the test results are reported in Ontario. Water managers now have strict rules to follow, and government workers make sure the rules are enforced. Testing labs must inform the local Health Unit and the Ministry of the Environment if any contamination is found. Sadly, these changes are too late for the seven Walkerton residents who died, and the many others who still have health problems. Sicknesses like irritable bowel disease, high blood pressure and a rare kidney disease are found in Walkerton residents at a much higher rate than the rest of Canada. They are witnesses to the fact that there are no shortcuts when it comes to safe drinking water and public health.

BIBLIOGRAPHY

The following books, articles and Internet references were used in research for this book. Errors and omissions are my responsibility. The personification of young Bruce Ryan, is a fictional character based on Bruce Regan who really did die in the mine explosion.

Books

Ballard, Robert. *Titanic, The Last Great Images,* Madison Publishing, 2007

Aitken, D'Orazio & Valin. *Walking Fingers — The Story of Polio and Those Who Lived With It,* Vehicule Press, 2004

Beattie, Owen and John Geiger. *Frozen In Time,* Greystone Books, 1987, 2004

Braithwaite, Max. *Sick Kids – The Story of the Hospital For Sick Children in Toronto,* McClelland and Stewart, 1972

Brown, Cassie. *Standing Into Danger,* Flanker Press, 1979

Cookman, Scott. *Iceblink: The Tragic Fate of Sir John Franklin's Lost Polar Expedition,* John Wiley & Sons, 2000

Eaton, John P. and Charles Haas. *Titanic, Triumph and Tragedy,* Norton & Co. 1986

Fleming, Fergus. *Barrow's Boys: The Original Extreme Adventurers,* Atlantic Monthly Press, 1998

Giudici Fettner, Anne. *The Science of Viruses,* William Morrow & Co., 1990

Gudgeon, Chris. *An Unfinished Conversation:The Life and Music of Stan Rogers,* Penguin Books, 1993

Halliday, Hugh A. *Wreck! Canada's Worst Railway Accidents,* Robin Brass studio, 1997

Hustak, Alan. *Titanic — The Canadian Story,* Véhicule Press, 1998

Kluger, Jeffrey. *Splendid Solution, Jonas Salk and the Conquest of Polio,* G.P. Putnam & Sons, 2004

Leyton, Elliot. *Dying Hard, The Ravages of Industrial Disease,* McClelland and Stewart, 1975

Looker, Janet. *Disaster Canada,* Lynx Images, 2000

Lord, Walter. *A Night To Remember,* Holt Paperbacks, 2004

Newman, Peter C. *The Company of Adventurers,* Penguin Books, 1986

Owen, Roderic. *The Fate of Franklin,* Hutchinson & Co. London, 1978

Pellegrino, Charles. *Her Name, Titanic,* McGraw-Hill, 1988

Pellegrino, Charles. *Ghosts of the Titanic,* HarperCollins, 2000

Rutty, Christopher. *The Middle Class Plague: Epidemic Polio and the Canadian State 1936–1937,* 1999

Troubetzkoy, Alexis. *Arctic Obsession – The Lure of The North,* Dundurn Press, 2011

Wells, Susan. *Titanic: Legacy of the World's Greatest Ocean Liner,* Tehabi Books, 1997

Williams, Tony. *Hurricane of Independence, The Untold Story,* Sourcebooks, 2008

Williams, Glyn. *Arctic Labyrinth,* University of California Press, 2009

Wilson, Diana. *Triumph And Tragedy In The Crowsnest Pass,* Heritage House Publishing Co, 2005

Wilson, John. *Discover the Arctic: The Story of John Rae,* Napoleon Publishing, 2003

Nanton, Paul. *Arctic Breakthrough: Franklin's Expeditions, 1819–1847* Clarke, Irwin & Co. 1970, 1981

Periodicals

British Journal of Industrial Medicine, "Lung cancer in a Mining Community", April 21, 1964. deVilliers, A.J. and J.P. Windish

The Globe & Mail, "52 Die in B.C. Airliner Crash", July 9, 1965

The Hamilton Spectator, "Reconstruc Plane Crash as Massive Jigsaw Puzzle", July 10, 1965

The Globe & Mail, "RCMP probe Possibility of Bomb in Air Explosion that Killed 52", July 12, 1965

Popular Mechanics, "10 disasters that changed aviation", David Noland, September 2007: p70.

Government Documents

Transportation Safety Board:

Main Gearbox Malfunction/Collision with Water Cougar Helicopters Inc. Sikorsky S-92A, March 12th, 2009

First Air Flight 6560, Boeing 737 Accident, 20 August 2011, Resolute Bay

Transport Canada Road Safety, Collision Investigations ASF5-1210 1997 Ford E 350 Super Club XLT Van Vs. 2005 Mack CXN613 tractor / 2007 Great Dane Super LT reefer semitrailer

Public Health Agency of Canada

Lessons Learned: P.H.A.C. Response to the 2008 Listeriosis Outbreak

Listeria Monocytogenes Outbreak Final Update: December 10, 2008

Online Sources

CBC News "Families mark anniversary of fatal N.B. hayride," October 8, 2008

CBC News "2 Resolute bay victims survived earlier crash,"August 22, 2011

CBC News "A Survivor's Story, Nunavut Crash Survivor," September 19, 2011

CBC News " 'They just can't get away with that,' Moms want charges laid in N.B. van crash."

CBC News "Father calls for coroner's inquest into Bathurst van crash," November 14, 2008

CBC News "Listeriosis Outbreak Timeline," September 11, 2009

CTV News /AP "Winter team travel leaves parents nervous," January 13, 2008

The Globe & Mail "Tragedy in Southwestern Ontario," February 6, 2012

The Globe & Mail "The testing of Michael McCain," August 23, 2012

Ottawa Citizen "Canada's Worst Road Accidents," April 19, 2006

The Toronto Star "Driver ran stop sign in crash that killed 11 police say," February 8, 2012

The Toronto Star "Listeriosis victims still awaiting compensation," December 8, 2011

Washington Post "Navy Honors 1942 wreck survivor (video)," September 15, 2010

Washington Post "Shipwreck survivor recalls how town altered his idea of race," September 15, 2010

Other Websites Consulted

Canadian Public Health Association, Health Heritage Research Service, The Encyclopedia of Earth, Encyclopedia Titanica, Journal of the Hakluyt Society, Maritime History Archive, Health Canada

ACKNOWLEDGEMENTS

With seventeen new stories and all the rewrites for this edition, there are many people to thank. First, I am blessed by a patient wife who encourages me to write when I could have been finishing and trimming the house. Shirley is my first proofreader who, in her clear-eyed way, always asks the right questions. Thanks to my sons Adrian and Dan for many days helping their old man, especially this last busy year. A twist of the throttle to my brother Erik who checked my Crowsnest Pass information and who has led me to good reads since I was six. Some of the best bits came from his suggestions and the loaded-up Kobo. A salute to old friend (and soon-to-be author) Col. Chris Shelley, who provided current information on helicopters and crash investigations. Keep on writing. A tip of the hard hat to Shawn Comish, ex-coal miner and draegerman, who gave me a better perspective on coal-mining hazards. And a warm thanks to Ken Cleverdon, getting on in years now, who shared memories of growing up with polio.

I greatly appreciate the help I got in research from Robert Amesse and staff at Quinte West Public Library and also from Sharon Bugg at the Brighton Public Library. Friends of mine also read some of the stories and added valuable insights; thanks to Robert Delint, Harold and Helen DeKleer, Sid Vanderwilp, Jim Snyder, and Dave Deur. My thanks and admiration goes to Erica Larmer, dedicated teacher, and her students Sol Boden, Nicolas Poulin, Gavin Locklin, Elise Hutton, Naomi Dunleavy, Alex Howard, Darcy Howard, Joshua Burnside, James Grinton, Eric Lawrence, Sarah MacDonald, Liam Conroy, Eric Lind, Liam Doran, Luke Doran, Trevor Merrall, David Archer and Autumn Archer who did a test drive of several stories at Goodwin Learning Centre. Also a big thank you, once again, to Kathryn Corbett and her classes at Stockdale Public School.

I express my appreciation to Nicole Mortillaro at Scholastic for a great editing job and for having patience with my rural Internet connection and word-processor woes. Scholastic has always had very talented people, and I have every respect for the designers, marketers and bookkeepers. And once again, thanks to Sandy Bogart Johnston who has supported many editions of this book over twenty-eight years.

Finally, I want to thank my mother, Anneke, who taught everything to us with a well-told story.

PHOTO CREDITS

Page 3: Brockville Special/Canadian Press
Page 9: David Lefranc, Abaca Press/Canadian Press
Page 15: Collingwood Museum/Town of Collingwood
Page 19: Montreal Star/Public Archives of Canada (PA116389)
Page 24: AP Photo/Burt Emanulle/Canadian Press
Page 39: Ian Jackson/Canadian Press
Page 46: Vancouver Public Library (1090)
Page 48: City of Toronto Archives (SC-244-2)
Page 55: Glenbow Archives NA-4279-10
Page 69: Halifax Chronicle Herald/Canadian Press
Page 80: Canadian Press
Page 85: Department of National Defence
Page 90: Toronto Star Syndicate/Canadian Press
Page 92: Jacques Boissinot/Canadian Press
Page 96: Tim Clark/Canadian Press
Page 99: Jacques Boissinot/Canadian Press
Page 111 and 115: Andrew Vaughan/Canadian Press
Page 122: National Archives of Canada C-057787/
Canadian Press
Page 131: National Archives of Canada/Canadian Press
Page 149: Louie Palu/The Globe and Mail/Canadian Press
Page 161: Kevin Frayer/Canadian Press

ABOUT THE AUTHOR

René Schmidt is a retired teacher and a graduate of York University's Creative Writing program. He is the author of a prize-winning novel, *Leaving Fletchville*. This is his fourth book on Canadian disasters. He and his wife live in Trenton, Ontario, while his sons travel the world and work at unusual jobs.